Education, Assumptions and Values

Brenda Watson and Elizabeth Ashton

David Fulton Publishers
London

David Fulton Publishers Ltd
2 Barbon Close, London WC1N 3JX

First published in Great Britain by
David Fulton Publishers 1995

Note: The right of Brenda Watson and Elizabeth Ashton to be identified as the authors of this work has been asserted by them in accordance with the Copyright, Designs and Patents Act 1988.

British Library Cataloguing in Publication Data

A catalogue record for this book is available from the British Library

ISBN 1-85346-333-7

Typeset by ROM-Data Corporation Limited, Falmouth, Cornwall.
Printed in Great Britain by the Cromwell Press, Melksham.

Contents

Foreword

Hardly a day goes by without the appearance of an article on the purposes of education somewhere in the Press. Others bemoan the absence of values in today's world, as writer after writer agonises over tragedies resulting from deprivation, violence or irresponsibility of one sort or another. There is general agreement that education has a corrective role to play. Indeed, the National Curriculum requires education to be conceived in the context of the spiritual, moral, cultural, mental and physical development of pupils at school and in society.

In this stimulating book, Brenda Watson and Elizabeth Ashton set out to help teachers recognise that the teaching of values can and should be part of subject-area teaching. As a University teacher of Geography (an Africanist and a Climatologist), I have no difficulty in accepting that all study, whether of the humanities or of the pure and applied sciences, must take place in a values context. Why, how and what we study is unavoidably imbued with value and values, but the pursuit of truth requires us to avoid preconceptions and prejudice. Minds must be open and, as the student or pupil listens, questions and reflects, breadth and depth of understanding of values and empathy with others can develop. In this process, the teacher must recognise the integrity of each individual.

Even the youngest child thinks about values – consider for example the child's concern for what is 'fair'. In this helpful book, the authors show how the life of a child can be enriched, and in some cases saved from tragic waste, by realistic yet higher expectations by the teacher than are sometimes found in the classroom.

By exploring the meaning of education and values, and the impact of the various '-isms' on our thinking, the authors guide the reader towards a theoretical appraisal of what can be achieved and the practical means by which it can be carried out. It is their suggestion that those more interested in classroom practice than in theory might start with Chapter 7 and subsequent chapters, but the early chapters, culminating in a wonderful exposition in Chapter 6 of what life and education are all about, should not be missed.

It has been a privilege to read this book before publication and to write with good wishes for its success. Whatever your diagnosis of what is wrong with society and education (and it is axiomatic that we shall not all agree on every detail), you will be inspired by this book. Most importantly, it will give courage to the classroom teacher on whom rests so much responsibility for the lifelong happiness of the individual.

Joan M. Kenworthy, B. Litt., M.A. (Oxon), F.R.G.S., F.R.Met.S.,
Principal, St. Mary's College, University of Durham.

Preface

'Going back to basics' is a phrase which has been much bandied about recently. Is this because people do not know how to move forward? And is that because they don't know precisely where they are?

This book concerns assumptions – what people take for granted, the basic starting-points which we all have. These govern our attitudes to the world – to ourselves, other people, the environment, cultural traditions, the arts, the acquisition of knowledge, science, and any possible purpose or meaning to be given to life. Assumptions control all that goes to make up our total outlook on life, our philosophy, our world view.

From our assumptions arise our values – what we regard as inviolably important and/or desirable. Often the link between assumptions and values is obscure. Nevertheless we can all be helped to reflect on those assumptions. When seven-year old Brendan, a remarkably perceptive child, told a student teacher 'Money is not important, it can't buy you love', his values were grounded in his perception of the world, even though mostly at a sub-conscious level, operating with assumptions drawn from his background. Because the teacher invited further reflection, Brendan went on to make some empirical statements of how the world is: 'Burglars want money, but some of them want love as well and they might think that money can buy them love, but it can't.' This shows how his understanding of the world had already given him firm priorities with regard to what is really necessary and important in life (see footnote).

The journey into discovering what motivates us is endless and of absorbing interest. It is also vital to the health of education. If this book can share something of the excitement of deep reflection on such matters, it will have achieved its purpose.

We believe that assumptions are not immovable and just to be accepted, but that there is evidence to weigh and the possibility of change and extension. We therefore invite readers to consider how far their assumptions agree with ours and what reasons can be given for and against them.

Chapters 1–4 examine the values and assumptions tending to operate in our society today, whilst Chapters 5 and 6 focus on the possibility of reaching trustworthy certainty by moving beyond the commonly expressed view that all reasoning is culturally conditioned.

Footnote 1. We are grateful to Andrea Irving, 4th Year BA (Education) student at Durham University, for this example.

The second part of the book moves closer to the classroom to discuss ways in which actual practice in school can be significantly altered in the light of this. Those readers more interested in this aspect might prefer therefore to start with Chapter 7 and subsequent chapters, and then read the more theoretical ones in their light. We would like to stress however that the latter underpin the teaching method and lesson content of the practically-orientated chapters.

In the practical chapters, the tasks are closely connected with the discussion and so have been positioned within the body of the text. In other chapters, the tasks are collected together at the end.

West Malvern and Durham
September, 1994

Acknowledgements

We gratefully acknowledge the invaluable assistance of a number of people in compiling this book, and especially the following:
Helen Gibson for such willing and efficient secretarial help including producing the typescript for chapters 2–7, Valerie A. Blackbourn and Betty H. Bradshaw for kindly reading the finished chapters and making helpful suggestions, and David Cantrell for help in navigating the mysteries of a computer.

Above all, we wish to acknowledge our debt to all the teachers, children and students, conversation with whom has informed our thinking.

A small part of the book appeared in *Education and Belief* by Brenda Watson, published by Basil Blackwell in 1987, but the material has been significantly refocused.

Chapter 1

Crisis in Education

For some years, the following notice was displayed on the bars of the Monkey House at Edinburgh Zoo:

> Please do not laugh at the monkeys. They have not all had the benefit of your education.

This book is for all those – teachers, governors, parents and students – who are concerned about education today, perhaps even in despair about it. The book provides a radical assessment of the present situation, but suggests positive steps that can be taken to enable what happens in schools to resemble more closely education, rather than nurture, skills-training or indoctrination. (Please refer to Task 1.1: Why (do we) have schools?)

We begin by considering the impact of schooling on particular pupils. The following three case studies are all based on experiences of the writers when working in schools. They all pose serious problems for teachers, not least because the problems of the pupils transcend current developments. As you read them, please consider whether these problems are relevant for education, or whether you feel that they need to be dealt with before education can proceed.

CASE STUDY 1: COLIN

Colin, as an eleven year old from a socially-disadvantaged area (his elder brother had committed a murder and his mother had attempted to hide him from the police, resulting in her being placed on probation whilst the brother was jailed) demonstrated considerable interest and ability in history, art and nature study. He was observant and full of curiosity. For example, when his class teacher was on playground duty she noticed some sycamore seedlings and bent down to see them more closely. Colin ran across the field to ask what she had found, and called for his friend to come and see too. The teacher explained about the seedlings, and left the two boys searching for more. On another occasion, Colin found in a story book of *Hamlet* a print of the Pre-Raphaelite painting 'Ophelia', and was fascinated by it. His interest caused others in the class to bring prints into school of Shakespearian characters, with the result that the class watched video extracts from *Henry V*, which had been provided by a pupil. Much work ensued. Colin frequently produced some high quality paintings and drawings, and was always given freedom to pursue his interests in the classroom freely.

However, when he changed classes, he was taught by a different teacher who had no interest in arts subjects, preferring instead to work on mathematics. She forced Colin to spend large amounts of time on mathematics, at the expense of what interested him, and he gradually became surly and refused to work at all. He was frequently found sitting outside the Headteacher's room, alone at a desk, because of his refusal to work in the classroom.

In the secondary school Colin started hanging around with the boys who got into real trouble and so he lurched through one crisis after another – truancy, shop-lifting, morose depression and drugs. The gloom was relieved by a single teacher who, like the junior school teacher who showed him the sycamore seeds growing, observed how perceptive and diligent he could be. This teacher abandoned the curriculum and, through extensive project work using art (which Colin was good at), helped him to regain some hold on himself in a precarious world.

CASE STUDY 2: CAROLINE

Caroline was a ten year old from a very violent home. Her three older brothers were in special schools for disturbed children, and she was very unpopular with others in her year group because of aggressive, forceful attitudes which ensured she was a leader, in spite of her unpopularity. Other children tended to go along with her leadership because they were afraid to challenge it. However, she had a keen interest in nature, and once told her teacher in detail about a seal she had found stranded on rocks on the beach near her home, and how she and her friends had managed to get it into the water. On another occasion, because she had noticed the classroom plants needed repotting, she came into the classroom early, dragging with her a heavy sack of soil which she had dug from her garden. During long lunchbreaks she was frequently in trouble, and the class teacher had to have much patience in settling her down when sessions began. She would challenge authoritarian attitudes in the school at any opportunity.

A student came to take the class for four weeks, and the Head asked the class teacher to teach a class whose regular teacher was absent. During the middle of the session, the class teacher received a message from a colleague to the effect that Caroline was in trouble. She had thrown a kilogram weight at the student during a lesson, narrowly missing his head. As a result, the girl was expelled, and became a pupil at a neighbouring school. She continued to be difficult, and is now well known in the area for loitering in shopping centres with adolescents much older than herself.

CASE STUDY 3: THE JOY-RIDERS

Two young men from a housing estate which was near to the school where one of the writers taught, had stolen a car for the purpose of using it not for 'joy-riding' or 'driving for the thrill of it', but to ram a shop window in order to gain access to the stock of electrical goods on display. The police gave chase. Before the two thieves had driven far they crashed the vehicle into a lamp-post and were killed instantly.

This incident provided a focus for the social trouble and unrest on the housing estate where the two thieves had lived. For five successive nights there was civil rioting and racial abuse on the estate, leading to many arrests. Later, members of the families of the two victims appeared on television and made attempts to defend the reputations of their deceased relatives. The middle-aged uncle of one of the young men said: 'Our XXX wasn't a car thief. He was a professional ram-raider. He went out that night on a job. Ram-raiding was his profession.' As may be imagined, these comments raised fury in the region. They also raised the question of how conflicting perspectives ought to be dealt with. The two perspectives in question were:

1. That taking a vehicle without the owner's consent for the purpose of breaking into a shop does not constitute a crime if you are a practised (i.e. professional) person at so doing; theft, or being a thief, is when you take a vehicle without a utilitarian purpose in mind.

2. That taking a car without the owner's permission is stealing, but stealing it for the purpose of 'ram-raiding' is even worse because one is, in fact, multiplying the offences committed.

The uncle in question, and some other members of the community, attempted to justify a life of crime on the grounds that the young people in question had no prospect of a job, let alone a car. They considered, therefore, that they were justified in stealing a car. as all young men are entitled to drive, and that they should be free to take one whenever they desired to do so and the opportunity presented itself.

Reflecting closely on the outcome of schooling on such children and young people, we argue for a radically different approach to education from that experienced by those mentioned above. We consider that unless the curriculum, and the way that it is approached, is allowed to be tailor-made for each individual, schooling can not only be a waste of time but actually damaging in its effects. (Please refer to Task 1.2 for further thoughts about the various definitions given concerning the purposes of education. Can you offer any alternatives?)

It would be easy for people 'in the real world' to dismiss such a thesis as silly nonsense – quite unrealistic in today's world. Such ideas easily develop along the following lines: that the remedy required – teachers who actually care about pupils as people and allow subject-skills and attainment targets to take, if necessary, a back seat – is not feasible in today's world. Everyone knows that we live in a market economy, and teachers must accept this and operate within its constraints, preparing the young for this world – tough, consumerist, competitive, information and skills orientated. Those who want to will still be able to pursue arts and leisure interests, but the serious work of the school must not give a high priority to these.

Yet even from that perspective, a thriving consumerist society requires many of the virtues significantly absent in Colin's home background and his own propensities as he becomes more and more bored at school. Almost all readers will, if asked, concede that even more important than getting a good job and having a life-style enjoyable to oneself, and not anti-social to others, is a sense of wellbeing as a person. That is, someone who is more than the sum total of the factors fed into him or her; someone capable of genuine personal relationships of generosity and friendship; someone concerned about justice; someone who can cope with the traumas and inescapable moods of life without sacrificing his/her real personality and individuality because of the stresses associated with playing the appropriate role. Increasingly today there is fear that the 'basics' of society are absent. The existence of sub-cultures in which values operate which would – if widely appropriated – signal the breakdown of civilisation as we know it, has not escaped the teachers nor the media nor the government. The joy-riding incident illustrates the issue very clearly.

In many ways it would be hard to devise a better scheme than the present (and past) educational system for producing apathetic individuals of stunted intellectual, moral and spiritual growth. In a situation of increased affluence and availability of medical services, combined with the relentless impact of technology on the employment sector, people who are basically bored and resentful sink into apathy or turn their suppressed energies into activities which are often anti-social.

If you think this hard to believe, try inventing a system to produce the bored individual. We did, and came up with the following:

1. All the time having to do what someone else has decided for one.
2. Being the subject of a carrot/stick approach to discipline.
3. Being at the bottom of a hierarchy.
4. Not being able to talk about, or even think about, on one's own, what matters most to a person, because of being so distracted and because there is no silence.
5. Having to meet other people's expectations, even if one has not the ability, temperament or knowledge.
6. Being at the hub of contradictory values presented by other people with no help in how to resolve these contradictions.
7. Being constantly assessed by those in authority according to how one matches up to somebody else's criteria.

8. Being expected to be competitive in a situation where there are many more losers than winners, and in which all become fearful of losing their place even if they have it.

9. Being put with others of all the same age.

10. Having everything compartmentalised – subjects, people, life.

DISCUSSION: How many of these do you agree with, and can you add more?

The above case studies raise some very important educational issues. Of grave concern to the authors is the predominance of attitudes such as those which caused such disruption in the life of Colin. He was not *allowed* to pursue his interests, not merely because the teacher was unable to help him, but because the subjects which he found exciting did not play a major role in the school curriculum. The importance of mathematics in the school curriculum is deeply ingrained in the educational system of this country, presumably because it is felt that the ability to calculate accurately is essential for successful living. The invention of calculators has not freed pupils from the apparent necessity of working through pages of sums manipulating apparatus in order to help them develop numerical concepts – in the belief that practical activities aid abstract understanding. The fact that the apparatus itself is an abstraction usually evades the notice of theorists, and generations of pupils continue to be bewildered by the subject as a result (see Note on p.10). For Colin, the result was a disaster, the effects of which reinforced some background conditions of rebellion against authority.

There follow some prototypes – which could be familiar to readers – of people in our society. There are, of course, many inter-related factors which influence personality development, including environmental, sociological and genetic influences. How far any one of them can be used to account for personal development is open to debate. Nevertheless, educators are *required* under the terms of the Education Reform Act (1988), Section One, to address the 'spiritual, moral, mental, cultural and physical development of pupils'. We therefore invite readers to study the following factors – all based on personal experience – and to reflect on them:

- the type of education these former pupils might have received;

- any ways in which education could have contributed towards the development of a more satisfying, generous lifestyle;

- the motivation which underlies the behaviour of each;

- how each person would be likely to respond to the statements in Task 1.2.

WHITE: has high qualifications and holds high office, either in law, industry, banking, education, politics or the church. Has a charming surface manner, but at meetings uses this charm to manipulate those who wish to curry favour. Is expert in the use of psychological and sociological games and will exploit his/her skills in their use to increase his/her own status by building up networks with him/herself at the centre.

GREEN: has no formal qualifications and states s/he never had the chance to get any. Is unemployed and draws benefit for the family, but makes a reasonable living by working casually at the dockside or on local farms. Leisure activities include going to the local pub, drinking, watching television 'soaps' and watching for a chance to make more 'on the side'.

YELLOW: has no formal qualifications and makes a living by petty, opportunist crime, even occasionally car theft and 'ram-raiding'. Has never had a job, and draws state benefit for him/herself and dependent children.

PURPLE: passed four/five GCSEs but could not attempt 'A' levels; earns an 'average' wage which supports dependents and allows for a moderate lifestyle. Lives quietly, watching television, going on family outings.

BLUE: has no qualifications and enjoys boasting about his/her toughness; makes a living by crime, such as stealing expensive cars 'to order' and by dealing in drugs. Manages to elude conviction by being sharp.

RED: has high qualifications which have allowed him/her to gain high office; refuses to be manipulated and constantly seeks honest dealings at meetings in connection with job in civil service/church/education/industry. Because of this refusal to be manipulated has become 'stuck', but friends constantly reassure Red it is worth it because of the personal dignity and humanity which s/he has managed to retain in spite of the low odds on this being possible.

ORANGE: has high qualifications but took a large salary cut to obtain the professional job s/he wanted, and is quite happy to remain in that position until retirement, since it provides the opportunity to broadcast things which s/he feels need to be said about the organisation of society generally.

How one thinks, comes to conclusions and selects personal priorities is influenced by many factors. If education is to be effective in enabling clarity of thought, it is the *received* curriculum – that which each individual cares about – that is really important, rather than the *null curriculum*, the *explicit curriculum* or the *implicit curriculum*. It is this concern which returns us to our opening section as we consider what effect schooling has had on some individuals (see Figure 1.1). We close this chapter by inviting the reader to make predictions of the likely outcomes of education on the lives of the young people referred to in this chapter. Are they likely to become similar to any of the 'colours' detailed above, or is a completely new development possible?

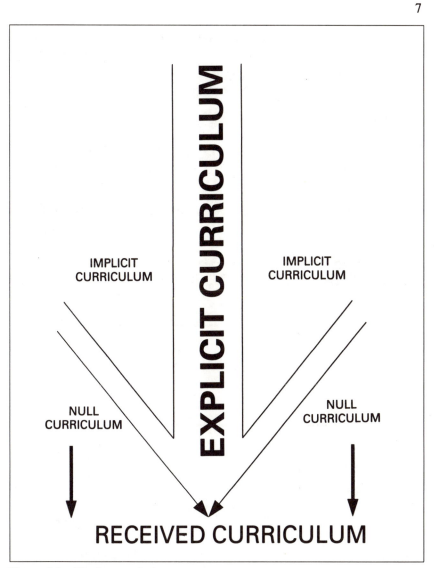

Figure 1.1   The four curricula

COLIN:

- Would you assess that Colin's problems were educational, sociological, environmental, medical, or 'what one would expect' from adolescent boys of the late twentieth century?

- For Colin, would subject knowledge alone be adequate for personality development, or would you consider other factors to be important? If so, which ones?

8

- For Colin especially, interests in certain subjects is very significant. How could these interests be developed in ways which would be educational?

- How would you like to perceive Colin's future? How confident do you feel in asserting that your perception is likely to be realized?

CAROLINE:

- How far would you assess education as having been helpful to Caroline?

- How confident would you feel in asserting that *subject knowledge alone* would have helped Caroline to develop more self-reliance?

- How would you summarise Caroline's problems, and the possible lifestyle which she will adopt in the future?

IMPARTING OF RELIABLE
KNOWLEDGE AND PROVEN
SKILLS?

DEVELOPMENT AS
PERSONS?

EITHER/OR
or
BOTH- - - -AND

THE NEED FOR BALANCE

We have RH and LH sides of the brain
Rigid demarcation is not possible
even physiologically, and far less in
everyday life.

We all do learn all the time through
the interaction of both. We cannot
indeed prevent learning - it's just a
question of what is learnt.

When teachers, or those who
control teachers, set a curriculum,
a syllabus, an assessment task, for
students, they are assuming they know
what is good / necessary / desirable
for students to know. They are setting

the agenda both by what they select
and by what they fail to select

The inevitable indoctrination this
entails can only be counteracted
through the twin development of
students' capacity for both LH and
RH brain activity.
Reasoning is required, but it must
be appropriately channelled.

To progress logically in the wrong direction
because the situation has not been
understood feelingly, is not only useless
but can be exeedingly damaging
depending on the nature of the
misunderstanding involved.

Figure 1.2   What is education about?

Overall, how many marks 'out of ten' would you give education for its efforts to help the above young people? (Please refer to Figure 1.2 after answering this question!)

There are many stories suggesting parallels between animal and human behaviour. Such comparison has always – through the medium of fable – been a favourite way of enabling humans to develop more sophisticated and mature notions of true humanity – a humanity which also embraces morality. Here is one quoted in a recent journal on philosophy:

> A lazy, improvident porcupine who has not prepared any shelter for the winter, asks if he can move in with a group of moles who, prudently, have worked hard to prepare their burrow. The kindly moles agree to let the porcupine in, only to find that they are constantly being stabbed by his quills. What should the moles do? (In an article in *Philosophy Now*, Winter 1993/4, pp. 9–11, Graham Haydon on *Moral Education* described by the editor as 'this year's hot topic'.)

We invite readers to:

- re-read the case studies, and perhaps consider others concerning pupils with whom you have had contact;

- consider what the moles should do and reflect on different approaches to morality and the way in which these can and should be shared with pupils.

TASK 1.1 WHY (DO WE) HAVE SCHOOLS?

Arrange in order of priority these possible reasons for having schools, and add any others you consider important:

1. To teach the basic skills of reading, writing and number.
2. To pass examinations.
3. To train people so that they can get a job when they leave school.
4. To introduce children to all elements of knowledge and a full life.
5. To help children to educate themselves – to begin a life-long process.
6. To indoctrinate the young into those values and attitudes necessary for civilised society.
7. To provide employment for teachers and to keep youngsters off the streets.
8. To ensure that the country produces enough scientists, industrialists and business people.
9. To teach people how to be good citizens in a democracy.
10. To inspire with a love of learning.

TASK 1.2 WHAT IS EDUCATION?

What does the word 'education' refer to in these comments?

1. 'He's not an educated person.'
2. 'Education is a life-long process.'

3. 'The education system in this country is a shambles.'
4. 'I think education is a two-edged sword.'
5. 'Schooling gets in the way of education.'
6. 'Why bother with education? It's a waste of time and money.'
7. 'Education alone can prepare us properly for the twenty-first century.'
8. 'The national budget should spend more on education.'
9. 'The last thing schools do these days is educate.'

Notes

Jenkins, S. (1994) Article in 'Rotten to the Core', *The Times*, 11 May, 1994.

Chapter 2

Schools and Values – the need for change

The art of progress is to preserve order amid change and to preserve change amid order.

These words of A.N. Whitehead – whose views on education are seen by some as more relevant today than ever – are a timely reminder of the need for both courage and perceptiveness. The truism that not all change is for the better is often forgotten, and *any* change is hailed as progress.

The need for change in schools is acute. Complacency is deadly, in education as in life, especially in times such as ours when so many factors call for great flexibility. Figure 2.1 highlights some of these factors, arising from advancing technology, but it is far from exhaustive.

Schools are like litmus paper, reflecting the state of society, and this places teachers in a highly vulnerable position. There is a great temptation for them to draw back from changes which might endanger their fragile status.

Today, however, change is being forced on teachers by outside pressures. These include direct legislative/administrative injunctions as well as the aimlessness and violence in society, and the apparent failure of schools to do much about it. Even more effective as a catalyst is daily experience at the chalk-face when teachers have to cope with the indiscipline of students, poor motivation to work, inadequate performance in public testing procedures, and increased truancy. Such considerations are predisposing schools to some re-thinking. Unfortunately this has often been at an extremely superficial level, without much conscious awareness of the values being advocated. A detailed look at one example, chosen almost at random, might be helpful.

A CASE STUDY

The staff in a British school were at their wits' end as to how to reverse a downward trend in behaviour and learning. Following a teacher's year's exchange in America, they decided to adopt an idea with which she returned, called the 'Self-Manager Scheme'. Yet the manner in which they applied it betrayed serious lack of understanding of the underlying issues – questions concerning the assumptions and values held by children, parents and staff.

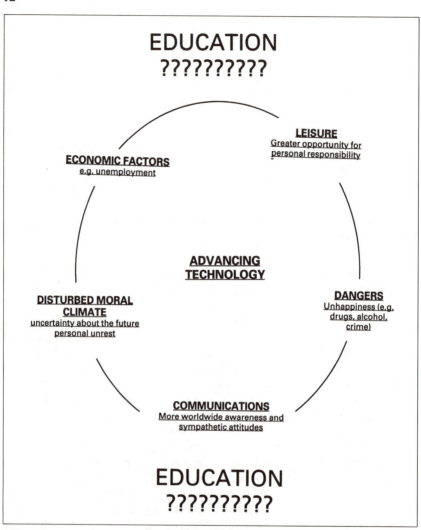

Figure 2.1 Forces for change in today's world

The scheme involved presenting yellow plastic badges to pupils who 'kept' for four weeks a set of rules drawn up by the staff:

- A Self-Manager keeps hands and feet to him/her-self.
- A Self-Manager is in the right place at the right time.
- A Self-Manager makes good use of his/her time.
- A Self-Manager obeys teachers and other adults.
- A Self-Manager keeps the school tidy.

Badges, which were to be worn at all times in school, could be taken away from 'rule-breakers' by staff, and the scheme sustained by rewarding pupils with extra-long playtime and opportunities to see videos or by penalising them, for example by debarring them from extra-curricular sporting activities and outside visits.

Results did not come up to the expectations of the initiators of the scheme:

1. Some children hardly ever kept their badge more than a few hours!

2. Children learned not to wear their badge outside the classroom. The chance was that the teacher they met would not know if they were a Self-Manager or not, so they could do what they liked and keep the badge!

3. The infant children, and some juniors, did not really understand the scheme at all, and did not know either the meaning of the rules or their relevance.

4. There were outstanding differences in standards among the staff. Some would withdraw a badge from a child for practically nothing, whilst other staff would immediately give the badge back again. The whole scheme began to lose credibility in the eyes of the children!

5. Some children said they did not want a badge – they had plenty of others at home which they bought from the shops! In any case they had nothing to lose, they said, because they were unlikely to get on to school teams.

6. Because of a shortage of 'good' players, non-Self-Managers were, in fact, allowed to be on school teams, and to participate in practices. This was because the members of staff responsible could see their team would be beaten without some of the tough characters who seldom retained their badges.

7. Some staff grumbled about those who were awarded a badge. Comments such as: 'X should never have got his, he was kicking Y this morning', and 'She'll not keep that for long', were commonplace.

8. Parents frequently came to complain about their child losing his/her badge unfairly whilst others retained theirs.

9. As the scheme began to run into difficulties the staff split into two sides. One side blamed the other for not trying to make the scheme work because they had not wanted it in the first place. This opinion was held by eight teachers out of fourteen. Since they were the majority, they voted to continue with the scheme and refused to carry out an evaluation. They felt the values, as expressed in the rules, were those which schools ought to be teaching. If ill effects were being produced on the ethos of the school, this meant the rules needed reinforcing all the more!

The staff had not engaged in any serious values discussion amongst themselves before putting the scheme into action. The majority were unaware, for example, of the manifold problems posed by the five rules. Procedurally, these rules were imposed on children – there was no idea of a discussed contract or covenant in which the children themselves might feel they had chosen to respond positively to the rules. And the content of the rules indicated the same dogmatic and authoritarian stance on the part of the staff. What is meant by the 'right place' and the 'right time'? Presumably that ordained by the teachers. The virtue of obedience is here being inculcated, with the presumption that adults know best. What does 'good use of time' involve? And who is to decide? Furthermore, the method used to inculcate these values was the stick-and-carrot approach, predominantly appealing to self-interest and competitiveness.

The scheme thus became a form of deception. It gave the impression of children being free agents who choose to manage themselves, when all the time they were being heavily pushed in a certain direction of obedience, conformity, tidiness, and, presumably, hard work.

Amongst children, attitudes to the scheme became clear. They demonstrated: procedural obedience to avoid getting into trouble; enjoying managing the system; a defiant or at any rate 'couldn't-care-less' attitude towards authority, and an anger at unfairness. The real concerns of children seemed to centre round a desire for survival and doing what appears to be necessary to ensure this.

Reasons for values investigation

The example cited above illustrates clearly the need for education in assumptions and values, for teachers as for pupils. At least eight reasons support a major commitment by schools to this aspect of education:

1. Society does not wait for consensus before transmitting values, and neither do schools. They convey values every day, knowingly or unknowingly, both at the more explicit level of what is taught, and at the less openly acknowledged level of how the school is administered. The latter constitutes a largely hidden agenda which determines, in no small measure, the content of the schooling experience. Education cannot be value-free. Undue influencing of the young in certain directions rather than in others is inevitable. Rather than being at the mercy of chance, teachers need to be as aware as possible of what they want to convey, and students as far as possible should be drawn into this awareness. Otherwise they are simply being either conditioned or indoctrinated.

2. The first ingredient of an excellent school, in which relationships are good and learning happens, is a shared value system. (Note 1, p.21)

    Tim Brighouse, when Chief Education Officer for Oxfordshire, went on to say that such a shared value system gives a sense of direction without which no school can operate efficiently. Shared values encourage vision. In underlining the importance of what the school is about, they help to develop – in all concerned – a proper self-respect. Yet schools often convey conflicting sets of values, such as the example discussed above. A community is unlikely to flourish when it sends out contradictory signals.

3. The discrepancy between verbal intention and actual practice is significant. It is often not easy to ascertain what values are being transmitted because of the distinction between what people *say* and what they actually *do*. Paying no more than lip-service to some ideal can be due to laziness, hypocrisy, or lack of understanding, as well as to other factors outside a person's or a schools' control. Such lip-service is therefore not infrequent. No sooner are values and beliefs mentioned than someone will remark tartly: 'It's what people do, not what they say, that counts'. The criticism is often expressed that schools are fond of high-sounding statements, but the way that they are run, and the content and methods used within separate subject areas, convey something rather different. Often administrative convenience is put above the personal needs of pupils, and high-sounding idealism is undermined by the attitudes actually expressed in the day-to-day affairs of the school.

4. It matters very much what values are held. The excellent school depends on more than having a measure of agreement, as Tim Brighouse noted on another occasion:

> Some of the shared value systems we have are quite pernicious and they can be successful in a kind of pernicious way. . . . Most of our schools beyond question have unspoken assumptions in their organisation, their timetable and their curriculum which reinforce individualism and materialism, and minimise the need for co-operation. (Note 2, p.21)

This is a challenging observation concerning British education. Many values indeed are being conveyed which more and more people see as wrong or at any rate questionable. These include attitudes such as racism, sexism, elitism, crass commercialism, and the cult of the ego. The welfare of society depends on the chosen values being beneficial.

5. There is of necessity something of universal significance about the term 'value', even if a subjective view of values is held. We cannot choose values as we choose a car, or clothes, or plants for the garden. They are not a matter of mere preference, nor even of what is personally important (in a way that music can mean a lot to some people, and football to others). A statement such as 'I value honesty and integrity' implies some kind of obligation laid not only on the speaker but on everyone – irrespective of whether they choose to acknowledge that responsibility or not. The problems of establishing what is obligatory in any but a subjective sense are challenging, and need to be reflected on in depth.

6. The need for diversity must be acknowledged. In any community there has to be some accommodation of differing points of view. Ovid's maxim: 'discors concordia' – agreeing to differ – points to a necessary ingredient of being civilised. To fail to acknowledge diversity is in fact to try to live a

lie. As has already been discussed in point 1 above, value-free schooling is impossible. What actually is communicated reflects values from many sources. As James Billington noted:

> Certain points of view accepted in academic guilds have become the values transmitted by higher education. Schools impart values under the guise of imparting none. That is a form of dishonesty corrosive of a healthy democracy, which requires a pluralism of values contesting in an open market rather than the pretence of no values at all. (Note 3, p.21)

Yet such contending is only possible on the basis of some viewpoints being held in common. These need to be clearly articulated and accepted by all, otherwise the element of proper disagreement and controversy will threaten the fabric of the community.

7. In real-life situations there is frequently a clash between the different values held by the same person or community. Freedom of speech, for example, may need to be curtailed where someone is defaming someone else's character. A hierarchy of values has to be established, and no institution can run effectively without agreement as to what is at the top of a hierarchy. Working out such a hierarchy is a process of accommodation which should not be a compromise, nor be seen as such – still less a matter of expediency. Rather, it should be a conscious choosing of priorities, based on the awareness that not everything can be done or agreed. The practical limitations imposed by situations must be acknowledged.

8. Values matter to people – they arouse strong emotions and provide long-lasting as well as immediate motivation for action. The personal development of children and young people needs a well-thought-out commitment by them to certain values. Such commitment is not an optional extra but vital for personal growth. It is not for schools to dictate a commitment to particular values or beliefs, but it *is* their responsibility to ensure that students learn *how* to reflect about such values, so that they can form their own authentic commitments from a basis of understanding and awareness rather than ignorance and insensitivity.

Schools therefore cannot escape the responsibility of wrestling with these problems and seeking to make explicit their agreed starting-points as yardsticks against which to measure practice.

The values clarification approach

Despite the above injunction, education in assumptions and values is frequently ignored, often because schools are unclear about how to do it. One approach which has however gained a considerable following is that of 'values clarification'. It was first formulated by Louis Raths, who in turn built upon the thinking of John Dewey (Note 4, p.21). A significant book, which set out the approach with practical strategies for teachers and students, was produced in 1972 by Simon, Howe and Kirschenbaum (Note 5, p. 21). The ideas there presented explain very well a view of the 80s and 90s. It notes that:

> Everything we do, every decision we make and course of action we take, is based on our consciously or unconsciously held assumptions, attitudes and values. (p.13)

and makes the further point that:

> The children and youth of today are confronted by many more choices than in previous generations. They are surrounded by a bewildering array of alternatives.(p.15)

For teachers to respond to this situation by adopting a moralising stance is counter-productive. 'Young people brought up by moralising adults are not prepared to make their own responsible choices.' Equally inappropriate is the *laissez-faire* attitude which ignores the real issues involved on the grounds that values are just personal, subjective matters. Instead, values clarification seeks to help young people build up their own value system. Its focus is initiating students into the whole area of decision-making, placing the responsibility for choice firmly in the court of students themselves.

The theory here is impeccable as far as it goes, but it is seriously insufficient, for in order to ensure that teachers do not attempt to over-influence students, the content of values tends not to be taken seriously.

> Raths was not concerned with the *content* of people's values, but with the *process of valuing*. He focuses on how people come to hold certain beliefs and establish certain behaviour patterns.

This is a serious weakness because content is unavoidably involved in the process of valuing. In reflecting on values it is not the fact that people *do* value but *what* they value that engages attention and can arouse heated debate in discussion with others. Not to address what fundamentally interests people in their own valuing becomes pointless after the initial sociological excursion.

A second reason why it is unsatisfactory to bracket-out the content of values is that to do so is not itself a value-free activity. The values clarification approach itself rests on certain assumptions, and those using it do not regard these as optional. It matters to them which values people hold. As becomes clear from p.25 of the book, the values clarification approach expects certain values to be put across and encouraged. It gives advice to teachers:

> When using the activities and strategies for values clarification, encourage a classroom atmosphere of openness, honesty, acceptance and respect.

Most people would agree, but the point is that these are values themselves which are often not practised because other values have priority for people. The extract goes on:

> The teacher (should) share his (*sic*) values, but does not impose them. In this way,

he presents the class with a model of an adult who prizes, chooses and acts according to the valuing process. The teacher gets a chance to share his actual values as does any other member of the class. The particular content of his values holds no more weight than would anyone else's; but his behaviour reinforces the seven valuing processes. (Note 6, p. 21)

Here again, the idea of no more weight being given to the teacher's view may give a wrong impression outside its proper context. The proper context is avoiding the authoritarian 'Because *I* say so it is so and you must accept it.' In that sense the teacher's opinion should not carry more weight. That is not however the end of the matter, because the teacher ought to have more experience, thought and evidence behind the opinions held.

Being value-committed itself, the values clarification approach must therefore concern itself with two aspects. The first relates to what people happen to value and the second to what is valued, for example 'justice' as a value. Attention to the first is legitimate in itself, but must not be allowed to go off on a life of its own without the second, otherwise it denies truth, reinforces relativism, and ultimately runs into a sterile backwater. Clarification must go further. It is not enough on its own. Values education needs also to embrace evaluation.

Beyond values clarification

The education in assumptions and values which this book is advocating takes seriously the criticisms which can be levelled at the values clarification approach. It acknowledges the importance of the non-moralising aspect, as well as the difficulties caused by the complexity of issues and the tendentious status of authority. It does however focus attention on the content of values, as well as the act of valuing. It therefore also openly acknowledges which values it itself operates on, without having to pretend to be value-free in its insistence that only process not content is the proper object of concern. Education in assumptions and values exposes what it takes for granted so that it can be openly reflected upon. It thereby avoids the charge of attempted inculcation of certain values rather than others. Besides this it permits a much deeper engagement of the issues in a way that can be seen really to matter to people, because it has not banned from the outset the possibility that at least some values may be obligatory on moral grounds.

A significant word omitted from almost all present discussion on values education is the word 'ought'. The possibility that there may be values which individuals/societies are morally obliged to hold, is normally never even raised; subjectivism tends to be assumed. With regard to what goes on in schools, it is important to note several points:

a) This view is often indoctrinated and not opened up for discussion. Teachers will often say, 'Now what do you think, and you, and you?', as they ask different students in the class. And then the teacher says, 'We all have our own opinions and we must respect other people's right to their own opinions, because we are not talking about facts but about our own personal ideas.'

The intention of the values clarification approach may not be to trivialise or leave the impression with the class that anything goes, and that there is no point in challenging what anyone else has to say. Yet this is often what is actually received. There is a crucial distinction to be drawn here between what teachers think they are communicating – the *explicit* curriculum – and what in fact students are receiving (see Chapter 1 for discussion on the four curricula).

b) The relativist kind of approach creates a cleavage between how in fact values operate in people's lives and how they are studied, for people do not think of their values as just preferences. Those who regard prejudice against people as wrong and worth making a determined stand against, do not regard the value behind anti-racism or anti-sexism, for example, as a purely subjective judgement. They assume the objectivity of the value perceived, namely that every human being is worthy of respect regardless of colour, creed or sex.

c) The assumption that values are entirely relative makes any discussion, appeal to reason, or attempt to convince another, pointless. If there is no evidence of any kind to be appealed to which can require consideration by others, and if reason is regarded as quite incapable of making any contribution to the values which arouse passionate feelings, then why bother to debate? If values are just subjective, then anti-Semites have as much right to their values as do anti-racists.

d) In the day-to-day running of a school, and in the way subjects on the timetable are taught, decisions have to be made, so certain people and their values will tend to come out on top in the values game. This may simply be on the principle that might is right. It is of paramount importance, therefore, that schools should raise the questions of whether there *are* objective values, and if so what are they, and if not what are the implications.

Implications for schools

To introduce work in depth on assumptions and values may involve asking far-reaching questions about whether the priorities currently valued in schools are those which *ought* to be. Are schools providing what young people really need to equip them for today's and tomorrow's world in a way that is wholly educational? If they are not, then courage is needed to rethink the priorities, perhaps in a very radical way indeed. It is worth quoting Gilbert Griffin, formerly on the advisory staff of Oxfordshire LEA, who had this to write about secondary education in Britain when he retired eight years ago. His remarks are just as appropriate in the mid-90s:

> If those charged with the responsibility for creating timetables for the education of our secondary school population could start with a blank sheet of paper, what would be the pattern of each learning week?. . . . Would our findings continue to construct a timetable of little boxes where the dividers defy anything but the most tenuous links between the subject so contained? Would the pressures of so many vested interests (university, employers, political parties, parents, governors, etc., etc.) mean that in the end we should be forced back to the mould which has failed us to a growing extent for decades?. . . . Young people want time to work out for themselves an adequate answer to questions of BEING. They deserve the opportunity to find a satisfying rationale for their lives. Questions of 'WHY?' need to be applied not only to the world of nature, of economics, or of demography, but perhaps more importantly to relationships and to ultimate questions of existence and purpose. Education needs to Satisfy. There may be reasons for education as a discipline to serve a useful function for the state and society, but above and beyond such aims must lie the nurture and development of the PERSON. (Note 7, p.21)

Unless schools take seriously this aspect of education, the values conveyed to children and young people are simply those of the adults who happen to wield power in the environment in which they grow up. The question then becomes *whose* values. This turns out to be a very complicated matter indeed, and one which, as regards this child or that, requires the acknowledgement of immense diversity. What can we therefore do about it? We can accept this and encourage schools to attend to the one person who needs to cope with the particular package of values presented to him or her – the child. Education needs to be radically personality-centred.

TASK 2.1 CONSIDER THESE QUESTIONS:

1. What do you consider are the values mostly put across today by:
   a) society as a whole?
   b) the home backgrounds of pupils?
   c) a school you know well?
   d) (if you are a teacher) your own teaching?
2. How are these values put across, or not?
3. Do some of these values contradict each other?
4. If you answered YES to question 3, do you think that pupils realise this?
5. If so, what is being done about it, either to bring the values into harmony, or to help pupils to cope with the confusion?
6. What about the problem of hypocrisy? Why do words and behaviour sometimes/often/rarely not tally?
7. Can people *choose* values?

8. Should the word *ought* be abolished in connection with values, or are there some values which really are obligatory for everyone?

9. Is there room in a community for disagreement on values? If so, what is essential for this to happen without the community disintegrating?

10. What happens when different values unavoidably clash, as they often do in real situations? How do we decide which values should give way?

Notes

1. Tim Brighouse, speaking at a conference at Westminster College, Oxford, March 1985.

2. Tim Brighouse at a meeting on Education in Beliefs and Values, held at the Farmington Institute, Oxford, October 14, 1985.

3. James Billington in Thomas Jefferson Research Centre Paper No. 214 Nov.–Dec. 1984 p.2.

4. See e.g. Raths, Louis E., Harmin, Merrill, and Simon, Sidney B. (1978) *Values and Teaching*, 2nd edition, Charles E. Merrill Publishing Co, Columbus, Ohio.

5. Simon, Sidney B., Howe, Leland W., and Kirschenbaum, Howard (1972) *Values Clarification: A handbook of practical strategies for teachers and students*, Hart Publishing Co. Inc., New York.

6. Ibid. pp. 13, 15, 25.

7. Gilbert Griffin in an unpublished paper discussed at the Farmington Institute, Oxford, 1986.

Chapter 3

Cross-purposes in Education

The word 'education' is used in ordinary speech with two quite distinct meanings. The first meaning loosely describes what schools, colleges and universities are about. Education in this sense is synonymous with schooling, or other forms of institutionalised learning. There is, however, a quite different meaning, one which is concerned with developing the potential of individuals to become persons in the fullest sense of that word. Schooling can only give impetus to the process, for education can and does happen outside schooling. In this book we are primarily concerned with relating the two meanings so that education actually happens in schools.

What is education?

The high view of education centres upon enabling people – in freedom – to gain knowledge and enlightenment as something worthwhile in itself. The benefit to society is seen as an off-shoot, which will come about through such individuals being balanced people whose presence and self-chosen involvement will help to create a healthy society. Education is therefore about helping people to think and act responsibly for themselves, and to find self-fulfilment and a quality of life appropriate to their own particular gifts, opportunities and insights. It is about promoting personhood.

Being a person may be thought of as involving a five-fold attitude of respect – for oneself, for other people, for the environment, for beauty and for truth. Together these form a creative circle. They may be seen as corresponding to the classical ideals of justice, beauty and truth, allied to the ancient maxim 'know thyself' (see Figure 3.1).

Here, the word 'respect' has a basic meaning of 'looking at' or 'paying attention to' something, and a further meaning of 'esteeming, honouring or valuing' something. In fact 'respect' is valuing in the strong sense of that word. Respect is the opposite of indifference and contempt. The five-fold nature of this 'respect' draws attention to the need for balance. Thus respect for oneself does not involve self-centredness; such respect would be inordinate because it

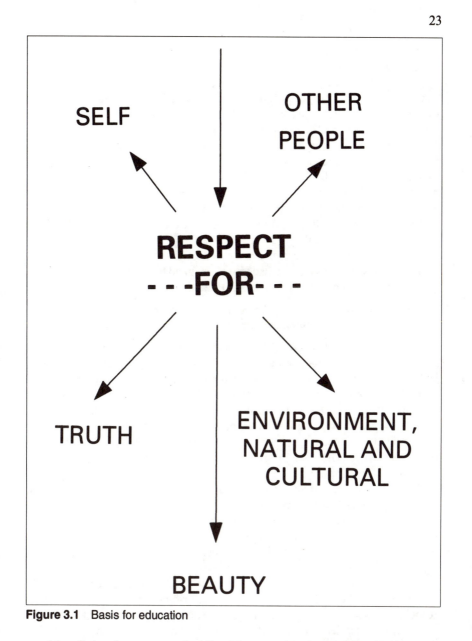

Figure 3.1 Basis for education

would exclude other aspects of reality. There needs to be a quality of all-round-edness, whereby over-attention to one aspect is corrected by being mindful of another. Exclusive attention for any one concern can lead to dangerous obsession.

Many people regard respect for a person as a person as axiomatic, yet this view can be challenged. The importance of affirming oneself and other people will form the subject of further discussion in Chapter 6.

Respect for the environment is twin-focused. It concerns both the natural world, and the world of human cultures. In neither sense is an affirming approach towards the environment a novel feature of the final decades of the twentieth century. Respect for the environment, natural and cultural, acknowledges that people are part of these worlds, each with their own autonomy yet powerfully influencing one another.

The word 'beauty' suggests a heightened awareness, and delight in qualities such as shape, proportion and colour which the environment – natural or manufactured – can display. Quite apart from the vexed question as to whether beauty is 'in the eye of the beholder' or whether it has objective reality, the appreciation of beauty has been one of the hallmarks of every civilisation.

Finally, respect for truth is fundamental. Without it there can be no respect for the self that one really is, for other people as they are, or for the world which happens to be in existence. Even awareness of beauty is, for most writers, artists and musicians, in a deep sense linked to awareness of how things actually are. Chesterton once spoke of it like this:

> The startling wetness of water excites and intoxicates me; the fieriness of fire, the steeliness of steel, the unutterable muddiness of mud. . . . (Note 1, p. 35)

The pursuit of knowledge – understood as the opposite of ignorance, blindness and delusion – is central to education and to being a person. It follows that a lack of emphasis on the search for truth is a serious omission. Yet this has been an unfortunate feature of much educational thinking in recent years, which has concentrated on relevance, meaning and description rather than truth (see Chapter 4, pps 46–49 for a fuller treatment of this issue). We need to raise the question whether meaning is *created* by us or *discovered*, rather than assuming one or the other, as in much progressive teaching on the one hand or dogmatic teaching on the other.

A person who genuinely pursues the five-fold attitude of respect will tend to develop certain traits of personality. There are many ways in which these can be summarised, as any search for shared values will show. In a nutshell, it can perhaps be expressed like this: such a person will have a quality of openness, characterised by enthusiasm, perceptiveness, integrity and a concern for fairness for all.

Openness is a tricky concept which will be discussed at some length in Chapter 6 – particularly the kind of openness which is properly educational. It includes openness to evidence, to further possibilities, and to new areas of experience; it can lead to an attitude of critical affirmation (see Chapter 6). *Integrity* is concerned with developing a self-assurance which is honest and realistic. It enables the individual to see the importance of being someone, as well as of doing things and acting roles. *Fairness* relates to the search for justice, kindness, generosity, and a spirit of co-operation. *Perceptiveness* includes imagination, awareness, the ability to see relationships, appreciation of beauty, and acknowledgement of insights. It denotes also the capacity to see behind false impressions or deception. *Enthusiasm* is of great importance as a

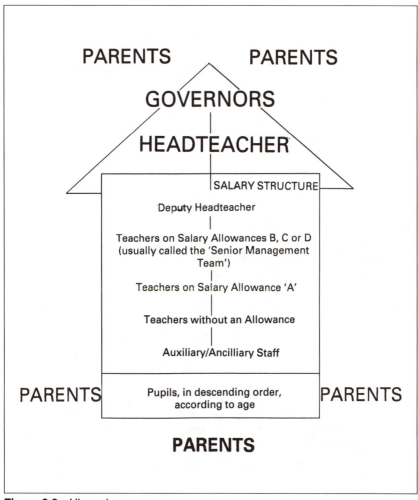

Figure 3.2 Hierarchy

major motivating factor in undertaking self-education. It is generated by attentiveness and shows itself in a heightened sense of wonder, and often in a capacity for humour.

The authoritarian structure of most schools

The outline presented of education as being a process whereby the individual is enabled to gain knowledge and enlightenment in a spirit of freedom is usually assumed to be synonymous with what happens in schools. Whether this assumption is accurate can best be judged by examining the structure within which most schools in Great Britain attempt to operate (see Figure 3.2).

Schools are commonly structured around a hierarchical system in which the Headteacher is legally responsible for the administration of the school and of the decisions made by all the staff working in it. A school hierarchy has existed since the notion of Headteachers themselves, with responsibility to the School Board/Education Authority and latterly with increasing (since the Education Reform Act, 1988) responsibility and accountability to the School Governors.

The increasing numbers of salary allowances during the late 1980s, which were intended to motivate teachers towards greater teaching excellence, have strengthened this hierarchical system. Whether this notion has been realised has yet to be discovered, but what is certain is that teaching staff on the higher levels of allowance are frequently found to comprise the 'Senior Management Team' which has regular meetings in order to decide on school policy. Excluded from this body are the teachers who have yet to attain an appropriate allowance, but who must attend all other staff meetings.

It is not difficult to perceive how such a structure is so easily extended to the children in the school, whereby the oldest are deemed to be higher up the hierarchical ladder than those on its lower rungs. However, how appropriate is this structure for the type of education which has been described and advocated as being truly *educational*?

What is reflected are the attitudes and assumptions underlying the Self-Manager Scheme which was described in Chapter 2. That is, that the adults working in the school know better than the children what is needed for them, and that such can be imposed upon them by the adults on the higher rungs of the hierarchical ladder. That such systems are open to internal politics – and no doubt external politics too – is only too obvious. It is vital to examine in detail the *educational effects* of such a structure on the quality of education provided by the many schools attempting to work in this way.

The over-riding assumption seems to be that someone must 'be in charge' – that some authority must be imposed from 'above' which will, at the minimum, maintain standards already achieved, and hopefully improve upon them. Hence, the authority may be envisaged as filtering from the Head and Governors to the Deputy Head and through him/her to the Senior Management Team, and so to the remaining Staff and then to the children. How helpful, however, are such assumptions and structures for helping young children take responsibility for their learning and through it provide educational opportunities for developing the five-fold respect as described in Figure 3.1.?

Nurture – that is nurture into the type of society into which the adults themselves have been nurtured – would seem to be the dominating value. Through the 'stick and carrot' approach (as exemplified in the Self-Manager Scheme and developed through the Senior Management Team) such internal school politics attempt to train children to live in a community which is envisaged as effective: that is effective in pushing children's efforts into classroom work which will enable them to proceed satisfactorily through the Attainment Targets of the School Curriculum.

Despite assurances in a recent publication (NCC April 1993, p.1) that the National Curriculum had been 'conceived in the context of the spiritual, moral, cultural, mental and physical development of pupils at the school and of society', the actual priorities governing most schools seem to operate against such holistic development. Who, for example, decides the form in which this 'context' is to be delivered? What are the structure and assumptions which underlie it?

That the nurture of pupils into 'society' is the focus seems to be the most probable answer to the latter question – with 'society' itself being envisaged as a type of 'golden age' which education is required to sustain.

How *educational* is the idea of nurture? Undoubtedly nurture of the pupils was the intention of the Self-Manager Scheme described in Chapter 2, but the nurture was an effort to condition children according to the values held by the adults in control and, as discussed on page 13, these values were not openly discussed.

Nurture and education: the 'enveloping' view

Nurture is one of three major ways of bringing up the young which the twentieth century has inherited, and which needs to be seen as distinct from education. It is the oldest and most natural of these.

Through nurture children are trained by upbringing, as well as by deliberate instruction, to follow in the footsteps of adults. Muslim children, for example, absorb Islam through their environment in the home as well as receiving it by direct teaching. This is an extremely effective method of influencing the young because it works by immersion within a culture, and by example. College and university students, for example, often find it extremely difficult to cope with freedom because of the effect of conforming to the kind of nurture they received.

Nurture in some sense is inevitable because children are bound to be influenced by the adults in their environment. Deliberate nurture is generally part of what responsible parents and adults do, those, that is, who really care for and delight in their children. In the modern world, however, because of uncertainty concerning culture, beliefs and values, and also considerable break-up in family and social life, the systematic nurture which used to be the norm is becoming rarer.

The relationship between nurture and education is complex and the two concepts should not be equated. Nurture can be the cradle of education, when it is conducted in a way which enables growing children to question and reflect upon how they are being brought up. It can, however, be simply another word for conditioning, having the effect of closing doors and producing tunnel vision. It can leave its recipients at the mercy of tradition, fortunate or unfortunate as this may be, unless accompanied by and extended into education. By building on nurture, education must seek to open up vistas beyond nurture.

Nurture of the right kind is of immense value in promoting education. But what do we mean by 'the right kind'? If your reaction to this is, 'There is no right kind', please turn for a full discussion to Chapters 4–6 especially pp.70, 76. Here we are arguing that, if the fundamental values behind 'education' as discussed above are accepted, then certain aspects of nurture are appropriate.

We need to be *treated* as people before we can begin to develop our potential as people for ourselves. Teachers and psychologists constantly draw attention to the crucial role played by adults in a child's earliest years. A child deprived of love and security is handicapped for life. Systematic nurture, even of an educationally unenlightened kind, can – and usually does – provide this love and security. The child is the subject of attention from adults who care for it and who wish to pass on what they feel is meaningful and important. The child is therefore brought into living conversation with other people, and has a chance to grow in the ability to make relationships. Casual nurture, however, can be damaging; the child may feel neglected, unloved and unable to trust anyone. Such a child will not easily develop a proper self-respect, and the journey towards becoming at all educated will be a long and arduous one.

Ideally, nurture should be characterised by another feature, namely an interesting and stimulating environment, in which the child has sufficient space and freedom to explore and to begin to make independent assessments and decisions. This is where much systematic nurture fails. It is too narrow, restricting and adult-bound. The child should be able to turn to loving adults, but should also have the freedom to be alone and enjoy discovering with his/her growing powers of awareness unfettered.

It would not be true to say that education cannot happen unless this right kind of nurture has prepared the ground. Fortunately later experiences can remedy much of the deficiency, which is why schooling can be crucial. Even one teacher can make an immense difference. The example of a ten-year old girl whom one of the authors once taught offers a useful example: the girl came from a vicious home background. On a school trip to the beach at Bamburgh, when the children were given freedom to paddle, dig in the sand, etc., she said, 'This is more like a real family than a school'.

The great support or impediment to education which different types of nurture can give needs to be underlined. Indeed, the two features of good nurture outlined above form part of the educator's role (see Chapter 7). The necessary difference between nurture and education is that in the former the focal-point for the adult is bringing the child up in a particular lifestyle, while in education the focal-point is the child's self-fulfilment as a person – a process which may, and usually does, involve criticism and perhaps abandonment of at least part of the nurtured lifestyle.

A utilitarian approach to education: the 'commodities' approach

A second pattern for bringing up the young, which should not be confused with education, may be termed the *instrumentalist* or *utilitarian* model. Historically this derives from the school of philosophy founded in the late eighteenth century by Jeremy Bentham, but its most usual modern form is rather different. Today the emphasis is on training young people to take their place in the world of work, and in creating prosperity. Society must be run efficiently and people must fulfil appropriate functions. Schools must be judged by their effectiveness in producing competence and a sound pragmatic attitude to life. Material and scientific performance is stressed, together with values conducive to such ends, which include industry, ingenuity and social responsibility. It is sometimes dubbed a philosophy of instant results.

Such an approach chimes in readily with the needs of our technological society, just as its historical forerunner was a response to the Industrial Revolution. This is not as heartless a model as caricaturists would have us believe. The philosophy behind Utilitarianism rates happiness and harmony as the end product. Without a stable society, life is in fact, as the seventeenth century philosopher Hobbes said: 'nasty, brutish and short'. J. S. Mill, a leading Utilitarian thinker, believed in education as a means of improving the quality of human life as a whole – including its personal, cultural and aesthetic dimensions. Modern advocates of the philosophy also maintain that people who know where they are, and who contribute effectively to their society, are in fact happy and fulfilled at a personal level. Incompetence, lack of structure and absence of direction are the fertile soil for deep unhappiness.

As a protest against the perennial danger of academic escapism, the utilitarian approach has something valuable to say. The 'ivory tower' mentality is proverbial. Many, both in schools and in institutions of higher education, pursue (and teach others to pursue) learning as though on some desert island, without much sense of responsibility to the people on whom they depend. It is reasonable to suppose that individuals who benefit from what society gives them should contribute to that society. Often they do not, and go off on a whirl of their own.

At a much more mundane level, the problem of motivating students in schools has forced educationalists into talking about 'relevance'. People learn better if they can see the point of what they are supposed to learn, and a clear, down-to-earth, measurable objective seems to fulfil this condition.

There is a grave danger, however, that the instrumentalist or utilitarian approach may be over-stressed. Indeed, it has always been strong behind the scenes. Those concerned with learning for learning's sake have had to wrestle with its presence in schools, colleges and universities ever since the great expansion of educational systems in the nineteenth century.

Many recent statements concerning schools have knowingly or unknowingly conveyed ideas far removed from the main concerns of education. This is no new development. An example of the kind of thinking powerfully at work, chosen almost at random, might be the Department of Education and Science document *Curriculum 5–16* issued in January 1984. Despite an appearance of educationally impeccable aims and objectives, the *real* beliefs advocated in that document may be expressed in quite different terms, harsh as it may seem:

30

- that economics is the key to life;

- that technology can control the future;

- that people matter chiefly in so far as they work;

- that the arts, humanities and religion are to be seen largely as pleasant extras, to be accommodated if there is time;

- that there is either no spiritual side to life, or if there is it is unimportant and secondary;

- that in the end there is only matter, money and the industrial machine.

The attitudes behind it are firmly entrenched in the educational system of the 1990s. Such an approach is not education. As Roger Scruton has tersely commented: 'Education, unlike prosperity, is an end in itself'. He went on to liken education to friendship:

> Friendship is unquestioningly profitable. However, you must never value friendship for the profit that it brings. To treat friendship as a means is to lose the capacity for friendship. Your companion is no longer your friend when you begin to weigh him in the balance of advantage. So it is with education; the profit of education persists only so long as you don't pursue it. (Note 2, p.35)

Education should indeed be mindful of the needs of society, and of the individual who must live in that society, and it should seek to accommodate immediate as well as more seemingly remote relevance into its curriculum and structures. We are concerned that school education often seems to present so-called bodies of information to students in ways which over-simplify the issues and do not engage pupils in in-depth discussion and thought about them.

An artificial divide between the worlds of learning and everyday life has been, and is, pernicious, depriving the one of realism and the other of vision. The challenge of the utilitarian approach may serve as a corrective, restoring a lost balance. But when the utilitarian motive takes over, education cannot be itself and cannot offer its real gifts to the world of work. We are concerned that school education often seems to present so-called bodies of knowledge to students in ways which over-simplify the issues and do not engage people in in-depth discussion and thinking about them.

The arrival of the National Curriculum in England and Wales has not guaranteed any improvement in this respect. Its stated context – that of concern for personality development – appears encouraging, but when we turn to the documents of the National Curriculum Subjects we are faced with formidable lists of so-called 'facts' and 'skills' which children are required to acquire throughout the years of their 'education'.

In actual practice the real values encouraged by the National Curriculum would seem to stem from a 'utilitarian' approach to schooling which effectively ignores other dimensions, or relegates them to the end of a long queue for time, resources, staffing etc.

It is often implied that the responsibility is the teacher's for such overall personality development, but it is reasonable to expect that the total structure and context in which the teacher operates should be supportive rather than pulling in another direction. Attainment Targets, assessment procedures in all subject areas, and so forth, give the impression of being written in isolation from such considerations.

There seems little doubt that the underlying values are that pupils should learn, as a matter of priority, the 'facts' and 'skills' as set out in the National Curriculum documents. Furthermore, the progression which has been built in to the material provided reflects the hierarchical structure which was subsequently forced upon the teaching staff, and which is reflected in turn by salary scales. Thus, the utilitarian model of education would seem to have been paramount in the planning of the National Curriculum, with the concept of 'nurture' being a phenomenon envisaged as the means of 'bonding' the whole system.

Of grave concern is that such concepts of education very easily slide, albeit unintentionally, into a system of conditioning, or even one of indoctrination.

Indoctrination and education: the blotting-paper view

The word *indoctrination* tends to produce very varying responses:

1. Some people say that it is inevitable – all teaching is indoctrination and there is nothing wrong with that. Teachers have to tell pupils what is the case and share content of knowledge.

2. Some see it as anathema – the very antithesis of education to be avoided at all costs in order to preserve the autonomy of the pupil.

3. Some see it as applicable only to precise beliefs, values and ideas which are intentionally put across in such a way as to make it difficult for the recipients to disagree. Because confined to occasions of explicit and deliberate purpose, such people usually limit the possibility of indoctrination to religious or political dogma.

4. Some see it as concerned predominantly with results. The intention to indoctrinate is not what matters, but what is received and how it feels to the recipient, and the effect of 'closed mindedness and restricted sympathies' (to use Basil Mitchell's telling phrase), which it produces (Note 3, p.35).

5. Some see it as most usefully discussed in connection with the specific content of beliefs and values, yet as inherently related to the wider conditioning which affects everyone. Indeed they would argue that content is more effectively indoctrinated the less attention is drawn to it and the more subtly it is put across.

We would argue for understanding the word 'indoctrination' in the fourth and fifth senses. The first sense virtually equates teaching with indoctrination and therefore we need another word to describe illicit forms of teaching which restrict the students' capacity to reflect.

The second way of looking at indoctrination (see list above) is also an unrealistic one. As an ideal it may be fine, but in practice the content of beliefs and values is inevitably impressed upon the young and the gullible. There is no such thing as neutrality, (see p. 71 for more discussion of this). Similarly, the notion of autonomy is a difficult one, subject to many philosophical questions. The idea of its being the supreme value has already been contested, and is increasingly contested today (Note 4, p. 35).

The question of intentionality (see point 3 above) is not adequate because harm can be done to pupils whether or not it was intended: the road to hell is paved with good intentions! Furthermore, it is not just a question of religious and political indoctrination about which it may be easy to be more specific. There is the question of the general and quite inescapable indoctrination of ideas. The classic examples of intentional indoctrination in the twentieth century have been in countries dominated by Communism and Nazism, but there has been attempted ideological manipulation within other countries too. Awareness of this should not blind us to the much more ordinary, normal indoctrination of pragmatic values which happens most of the time (Footnote 5).

The fourth and fifth ways of looking at indoctrination (see list above) together offer a more comprehensive view which draws attention to the real import behind the use of the word: one which concerns result and content (see Figure 3.3).

Indoctrination is the opposite of education because, whether deliberately or not, it bypasses the autonomy of the individual. People are inwardly taken over, and their thoughts and behaviour programmed according to the particular viewpoints, or ideology, favoured by the communicators. Indoctrination works by sending the mind effectively to sleep, so that what is impressed upon it is soaked up as by blotting paper. As such, it is important to note that even reasons for a given idea can be indoctrinated.

This particular point about indoctrination deserves more prominence than it is usually given. Indoctrination operates most efficiently when there is a failure to draw attention to other ideas and other areas of experience. What is presented therefore tends to be seen as comprehensive and complete in itself without the need to consider other possibilities. The indoctrinated person is completely unaware of the validity of genuine questioning and reflectiveness.

Hence indoctrination is often a by-product even of the right kind of nurture (see p. 31). If nurture is conducted without due regard and sensitivity to the awakening maturity of the child as a person in his or her own right, then it has a claustrophobic effect upon the child's development. Many 'good' parents and teachers, who think that they are doing their best for their children, are perplexed by the fierceness of the rebellion on their hands. This is usually a sign that well-meaning nurture or teaching has become unintentionally and

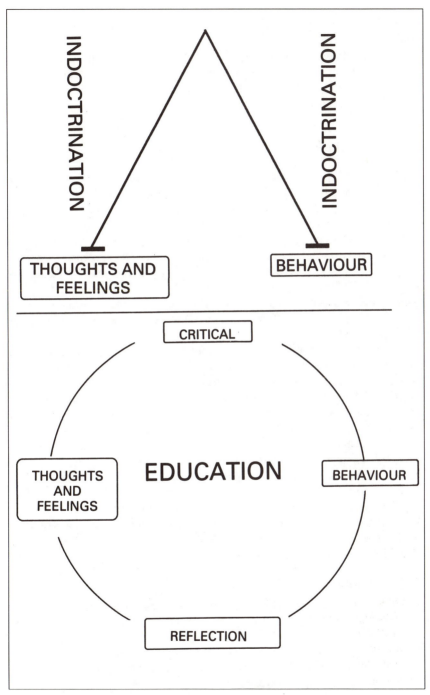

Figure 3.3   The difference between indoctrination and education

subtly indoctrinatory. As the recipient becomes aware of this s/he struggles to break free.

Similarly, it is chiefly through the *omission* of other considerations that the utilitarian model can become a form of indoctrination. An almost exclusive concern with the 'nuts and bolts' of existence can so powerfully distract people that they never reflect upon wider issues.

The need for clarity

The understanding of education outlined above needs to be expressed in a positive way which clearly acknowledges the assumptions and values on which it is based. So much attempted education fails because those called upon to implement it do not thoroughly appreciate the nature of the educational goal and the appropriate way to it. Education often deteriorates into a vague do-it-yourself approach, where young children and older students seem to be left to their own devices. Such an approach is a gross travesty of the educational ideal. It is also unrealistic. In the vacuum created by such inadequate notions, even though the rhetoric of fully educational aims and objectives may be retained, recourse is often made, in practice, to the other models for bringing up the young.

Our educational institutions reflect a number of attitudes. There is usually some attempt at education, mixed with some nurturing in consciously traditional beliefs and values, with here and there some deliberate indoctrination by enthusiastic individuals – especially in those subjects which most lend themselves to it. But the framework, especially in secondary schools, is largely governed by administrative convenience, over-specialisation, fragmentation, competitiveness, assessment-orientation and an impersonal atmosphere. This all serves to impose a largely unintentional form of indoctrination into a utilitarian approach to life – despite noble efforts to overcome the worst effects of these systems in the interests of real education.

The next chapter will turn to an investigation in depth of the underlying assumptions prevalent in our society which have encouraged such a state of affairs. It will do so by taking up the concern voiced in Chapter 2 of the need for a different approach to thinking about values.

TASK 3.1 QUESTIONS FOR DISCUSSION

1. Mark Twain is said to have complained: 'My education was interrupted by my schooling.' Would you say that is true in your own case, or in the case of any people you know?

2. How do you think a cross-section of the people you come up against in the course of a working day view the purpose of schooling?

3. How do *you* see the purpose of schooling?

4. Is Figure 3.3 clear in conveying the distinction between indoctrination and education? If not, can you suggest an improvement?

5. Do you agree that education can be distinguished from indoctrination in this way, or is this too clear-cut a demarcation?

TASK 3.2 SCHOOLS AND PRIORITIES

Arrange the following miscellaneous words in such a way as to indicate what you think the priorities of a school ought to be.

REFLECTING   BREADTH   PRECISION

                      FACT

STORY   ARTS

        TESTING   IMAGINATION

                    FEELING NO GOOD

AUTONOMY   EMPATHY

              SCIENCES

PROOF

              HUMANITIES   DEPTH

INTELLECTUAL CAPACITY

                            CLEVERNESS

CAPACITY FOR   AWARENESS OF
QUIETNESS   UNAVOIDABLE   CAPACITY TO COPE
                  IMPRECISION   WITH FAILURE

BEING A KNOW-ALL   THINKING
                             SKILLS

    WISDOM   SUCCESS

Notes

1. We are indebted to Charles Barnham for this quotation.
2. Roger Scruton in an article in *The Times* 12 June 1985.
3. Basil Mitchell (1970) 'Indoctrination' in *The Fourth R*, SPCK, p. 358.
4. Piaget, Kohlberg and others have seen autonomy as the highest point of moral development. This has been severely challenged by many e.g. Basil Mitchell, Olivera Petrovich et al.

Chapter 4

Underlying Assumptions

Most people are likely to agree that a major aim of all education should be to encourage balanced, critical thought. To do so, however, requires some terms of reference, some independent means of testing assumptions. How can we handle, for example, the following statement of values: 'Stealing a car for ram-raiding is not really stealing because ram-raiding is skilled. It is a profession'? So argued relatives and friends of the two ram-raiders who were killed in an incident on the Meadowell Estate in Newcastle in 1991 (see Chapter 1, page 3).

Study the following conversation, relating to that comment, between a Head-teacher (A) and two members of staff (B and C).

A: Of course you have here the clash of a sub-culture with the dominant culture. These youngsters were brought up with a different set of values. Through assertive discipline in the school we've got to change those values.

C: It's interesting that you don't say that what they did was wrong. Why was that?

A: Well, people can argue until kingdom come upon what's right and wrong. Better to use language which everyone can agree with. Besides, who are we to say what's right?

B: I should have thought that it was obvious that stealing is wrong, damage to property is wrong, and endangering people's lives is wrong. It's not just anti-social.

A: We say it's wrong, that's all, because our society depends upon people not doing that sort of thing normally. But during the war of course people were taught how to do such things and got MBEs for it!

B: Well, that's just the context – if you're trying to win a war. . . .

A: That's just my point. So-called morality is context-based – culture and sub-culture based.

B: So why are you disapproving of the ram-raiders? After all, they were only applying the values they were brought up with.

A: I've already said: because they're anti-social.

B: According to your definition of social, which is due to how *you've* been brought up.

A: Yes, and the vast majority in our society, which is grounds enough for seeking to enforce our view of what's anti-social.

B: I see. What's right or wrong depends on what the majority think?

A: No. I am just saying that in this case – the ram-raiders – the majority in this country think it's anti-social and should be stopped, and so we should do what we can to stop it. There's nothing illogical in that.

B: But if the sub-culture took over and became the dominant culture, would you accept your need to change your values to fit?

A: No, because I've been brought up with these values.

B: But you want to change the ram-raiders' values?

A: Yes, because it's a straight clash of values.

B: And you consider that your values are more right than theirs?

A: Well, in my eyes yes, but that's just how I and the majority in our society see it. We could see it another way.

B: But why? On what grounds do the majority feel it fit to hold such values? Is it only to do with the protection of property, etc.?

A: Well, that's one consideration, but there are others – generally what makes life pleasant. But then you're back to the *soft* reasons of what happens to suit me or us – there aren't any *hard* objective reasons.

C: Hm. The problem is that the two of you are operating on entirely different assumptions concerning the meaning of words like 'right' and 'wrong'. B holds that they relate to universal categories – a 'moral law' as it were, whilst A considers they relate to people's ideas, themselves the product of how they've been brought up. In which case the way forward is to assert more strongly those ideas held by the majority in our society.

A and B together: Yes, we must just agree to differ. Discussion gets nowhere. . . .

C: That's not good enough. If there is such a thing as right and wrong we can't leave it like that. And if we care about society we can't either. Besides which, these two different assumptions that you take for granted are not as equal as you imagine. There's a lot more evidence in favour of one than the other.

A and B, a bit intrigued: Which one? What evidence?

Readers might like to consider what reply C could make.

The nature of the problem

In order to appreciate the problem it is necessary to do some deep digging to examine the roots of the difficulty. Using another analogy, we need, having come to an impasse, to retrace our steps to the starting-point. In intellectual terms this is what we take for granted – what we *assume* to be the case. If we have arrived at an intellectual muddle, then we have to try to untangle it by looking at what, intellectually, we take for granted.

The disagreement concerns a fundamental difference – indeed an incompatibility – in the root perspective on the world with which A and B each start. C attempts to offer persuasive grounds for a re-alignment of such perspectives – a re-adjustment of focus bringing the two sides into harmony. This task is necessary because attempts within the conversation to convince each other did not work. But when C appealed to the criterion of consensus – or at any rate of the majority-vote – B pointed out that this was clearly inadequate.

Implied throughout the conversation – almost inevitably – was an appeal to intuitional certainty by both A and B. We all display certainty; we can be, and are, sure about a huge number of things, rightly or wrongly. But being certain does not make it right. We may be certain that the train leaves at five minutes past the hour, when in fact it goes at five minutes to the hour! The certainty displayed by A and B was not by itself convincing, even though confident eloquence can be amazingly effective in the short term, as natural 'leaders', including dictators, constantly demonstrate.

The conversation as a whole, however, was both civilised and not trying to overwhelm through words. It was an attempt to resolve the problem through reasoning. Yet unchallengeable demonstration of rightness regarding issues of this kind is impossible, and 'reasonable' people can and do think differently, coming to different conclusions from the same data. Almost any social, political or ethical problem, such as how to deal with drug-abuse, whether to permit euthanasia, policy regarding the treatment of criminals, and so forth, can produce sensitive and intelligent comment on both sides of a divide. What was very apparent in the conversation above was the inability of any of them to make appeal to any commonly-acknowledged trustworthy authority. As Professor Richard Pring has put it:

> Part of the present moral and social climate is a distrust of authority, especially in the realm of values. Without an agreed tradition of values it is not easy to see how one can promote with confidence one particular set of values rather than another. (Note 1, p. 53)

Any appeal to authority today can and does tend to produce the response 'But why should we trust this authority? Other authorities say something different.' We have therefore to move further back to examine the basic grounds for knowing anything reliably. To do this we need first to understand what really is at issue so that both sides are talking about the same thing! This is not so obvious a point as many think. It is very easy to be misled by words which have radically different connotations for different people, but which appear to carry an identical meaning.

The theme of the disagreement between A and B can be expressed in the form of a question as to whether there is or is not a moral law to which human beings should respond. The Headteacher (A) assumes that there is not. What we call 'moral' responsibility is response to social conditioning and/or human reasoning. B, on the other hand, assumes that the 'moral' imperative which people find operating in their consciences is a reflection of the fundamentally moral nature of the universe – it is something 'given' to which we have to learn to respond sensitively and appropriately, and not something invented by human beings in order to make life together tolerable.

But do they understand 'moral law' in the same way? Is the Headteacher's reluctance to use the word 'moral' due to one or more misunderstandings concerning its meaning? At least three misunderstandings can cause trouble:

1. Many people tend to think of the moral law as some kind of entity cast in tablets of stone somewhere in the skies! Clearly this is an absurd notion. The moral law does not have physical properties of any kind. If it exists it is a spiritual reality which transcends our categories of time and space just as surely as it is operative within them.

   'Law' is in fact being used metaphorically in such phrases. Just as the term 'scientific laws' does not refer to some written static code to be rigidly applied, but rather to the way in which patterns can be discerned within nature, so talk of the moral law refers to the inherent ordering of relationships in such a way that they are conducive to attaining what is just and fair.

   Unlike the so-called 'laws' of science, at least as understood within Newtonian physics, the moral law – if such exists – requires our co-operation in the creation of what will be. Human beings, and maybe also other living creatures, have been given freedom to choose in some measure how they live, and how they relate to each other. But such freedom carries responsibilities. If it is used in such a way as to cause harm to others – or indeed to oneself – then retribution will certainly follow. The moral imperative points to how justice will finally prevail; people cannot ultimately act unjustly and unfairly with impunity.

   There is a chain reaction resulting from any action, either creative or negative. If someone smiles at you or listens to you etc., it makes you feel good; if they speak roughly to you or ignore you, it pulls you down. It has often been observed that people tend to create the reactions which they receive – that life holds up a mirror to the self; treat people with contempt and they will tend to treat you back with contempt.

But the moral law is more than this cause and effect. It signifies that the world is created in such a way that certain attitudes and ways of behaving are appropriate and others are not, regardless of any immediately discernible consequences. What we are and what we do is measured up against a criterion of fairness or justice which is inexorable because it is not in our power to make or alter it, only to accept or ignore. Various Greek myths have drawn attention powerfully to the sense of fate and judgement operating on a cosmic level. Such a sense is diminished today, and the rest of this chapter and the next will suggest some reasons why.

It is interesting to reflect that talk of the moral law may have an immediate reflection in so-called laws of nature. For example, zoologists say there is no such thing as a natural man-eating tiger. Tigers only become man-eaters because of negative experiences of human beings, and in consequence learn to be vicious. Perhaps threatening behaviour towards animals causes a break with the moral law?

The way in which the moral law is expressed in words will obviously vary according to the specific cultural background from which people come. But words are in any case only pointers towards what they signify. And there are many ways in which the stars can be pointed to.

2. A second widespread misunderstanding arises from confusion between the reality of basic principles of justice and fairness with the enormously difficult and complex task of applying them within concrete situations. These are almost always unique, and deciding how to act morally within them requires great sensitivity and perceptiveness. It is most definitely not a case of applying a rule in some straight-forward rigid manner, because so many factors have to be taken into account. *Phronesis* is what Aristotle called the task of matching theory with practice within precise and particular circumstances (Note 2, p. 53).

Talk of the moral law is therefore not to appeal to a textbook of rules – fundamentally a very static notion – but rather to draw attention to basic parameters for the study of what to do. It relates to overall considerations which, although we may in our day-to-day decision-making ignore them, will nevertheless in the end apply; one's actions are judged by them ultimately, not the other way round.

3. The difficulties encountered in matching theory with practice are the source of another area of serious misgiving about using the word 'moral' at all. Hypocrisy is one of those vices which most people in our society react strongly against. Traditionally, morality has been a prime arena for the display of high-sounding impressive idealism coupled with often sordid practice. It is so easy to pontificate yet so difficult to act according to our words.

An almost sub-conscious desire to avoid adopting a moralistic stance which is vulnerable to well-founded criticism of behaviour lurks behind much avoidance of the word 'moral'. Terms such as 'socially-beneficial', 'creative', 'positive' do not seem, as yet, to carry the same unfortunate connotations.

Awareness of these misunderstandings can at least ensure that we are discussing the same thing! Advocates of the moral law are *not* arguing for a fairytale, static set of rules unconcerned with the subtleties and complexities of real situations. They *are* arguing for the reality of a concern for justice and fairness written in, as it were, – using metaphorical language – to the universe.

With this clearly in mind, we can proceed to look more closely at the roots of the disagreement. The status of 'moral', except within a precise context of humanly-devised rules such as when playing a game, itself rests upon a very basic assumption. We can caste this in the form of a proposition as follows:

The word 'moral' is redundant and unhelpful; 'anti-social' is what it actually means.

Reactions to the above proposition that the word 'moral' is redundant might be as follows:

1   Yes, we shouldn't use the word 'moral' because reasoning about morality is inconclusive – there is no clear proof of the supposed existence of any moral law (positivism).

2   Yes, we should avoid the word 'moral' because if such proof is unavailable, we should doubt that it refers to anything at all (scepticism).

3   Yes, 'moral' is redundant because we don't need any other considerations than those contained under the term 'anti-social' to explain situations in which the word 'moral' is used (reductionism).

4   Yes, talk of 'moral' is inappropriate because such talk has always been relative to the culture or sub-culture in which a person is brought up (relativism).

These four reactions relate to certain commonly-held assumptions which constitute stances – denoted by the suffix '-ism'.

1. Positivism

The first is the philosophical attitude known as positivism. According to this view, the only knowledge which is trustworthy is that reached by logical proof or scientifically acceptable demonstration of evidence. The positivist stance is one of the long-term products of the so-called Age of Enlightenment in the eighteenth century, with its emphasis on reason, coupled as it has been with the tremendous expansion of the sciences since the seventeenth century. Its most explicit expression has been in the positivist school of philosophy which grew up in Vienna in the mid-1930s and made an impact in Britain through the work of A. J. Ayer and others (Note 3, p. 53). Although in its most extreme form it is largely discredited in intellectual circles, in a diluted fashion it is still very much with us.

2. Scepticism

Its reliance on scientific method goes hand-in-hand with the second -ism, 'scepticism', which has had so pervasive an influence in the academic and educational institutions of our society for at least two centuries. Common phrases such as 'You can't prove it' imply that you should be able to, and if you can't your opinion is nothing more than your statement, and is therefore to be doubted. Such sceptism is normally applied in a highly selective way i.e. restricted to logical or scientific norms.

The presence of positivist-scepticism has the effect of consigning everything which is not capable of being proved in some empirical or scientific way to the realm of subjective opinion.

3. Reductionism

The third attitude is one in which people do not just doubt something, or regard it as inconclusive, they re-interpret it. They find alternative ways of describing it with which they can agree.

This attitude can be termed 'reductionist'. It has the effect of 'reducing' accounts of people's experiences, for example, to that which can be studied in an apparently objective scientific way. Hence it not infrequently leaves out altogether what is at the heart of the experience, without making clear that it is doing so; it pretends to give an adequate explanation when in fact the most important aspect has been ignored or explained away. Sometimes this is described as *nothing but-ery*. An example is the view that history is nothing but politics and economics.

4. Relativism

The fourth attitude does not appear to be so dismissive of other interpretations. It argues that what a person believes is related to the circumstances of his or her upbringing; it is unintentional conditioning. Someone brought up in one milieu may speak about the plight of the proletariat and the ideal Communist society; another may speak about submission to Allah and reverence for the Qur'an because s/he has been brought up in that setting. If the Muslim had been born and brought up in a Communist family s/he would have been different, and vice versa.

Relativism is a way of handling the diversity of views which people hold on matters not amenable to straight scientific investigation, and matters which are therefore beyond demonstration. As the relativist sees it, everyone has a right to his or her opinion and as no one can prove they are right, however subjectively certain they feel, all opinions sincerely held by people are of equal validity and deserve an equal hearing.

It is important to notice that relativism is closely bound up with positivism, scepticism and reductionism which is its matrix.

These assumptions about knowledge support, and are supported by, assumptions related to daily life-style. The materialist, consumerist, competitive, 'busy' aspects of Western civilisation are more widely acknowledged than the 'intellectualisms' (even though they are not seriously challenged by those caught in their web) and have been highlighted by closer contact with other cultures and ways of life (see Figure 4.1).

There is increasing awareness today that such assumptions are not beyond challenge. Many people perceive that such a lifestyle is unsatisfactory and does not lead to high quality of life. Views such as 'There is more to life than matter', and 'People need time to be still' are beginning to redress the balance, but only slowly, because our society as a whole still gives priority to the assumptions associated with materialism. Daily living along such lines serves to reinforce the intellectual apologia for the lifestyle. If people spend almost all their time and energies on getting money, coping with economic and physical necessities and pursuing chores and pleasures, they will tend to think that this is what life is about. The same holds for the intellectual -isms. Whilst there is widespread appreciation of the insights within these -isms, there is also appreciation of the inappropriateness of their being raised into the status of overall principles.

Positivism and education

Positivism points to part of what is valuable in education. Scientific method and concern for what objectively is, quite apart from any subjective imagining, is important not only in the sciences but in many other areas as well. Yet if this poses as the *sole* reliable method of arriving at knowledge, it is deeply destructive of other ways of knowing. One of the most fundamental assumptions behind education is the importance of people as people. Positivism, however, acts against the possibility of taking people seriously as centres of experience. This affects even obvious examples such as predicting football results accurately on past performance when attempts are made to discount personal factors.

An example in which people are put at a lower level of concern than economic factors is when discussions take place in local government about siting supermarkets on the edges of towns. Planning criteria do not require local councillors to take account of people's wishes; of the human values necessary for maintaining a lively town-centre; the need which people have for beauty and for the natural environment, etc. These are regarded as completely secondary to such matters as the economic viability of the site.

Positivism, however, is being challenged by science itself as it struggles with a fresh self-understanding. Modern quantum physics powerfully reinforces the need for a more flexible attitude to scientific knowledge.

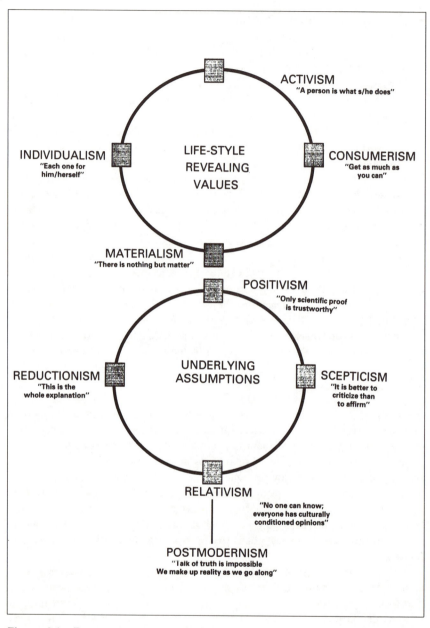

Figure 4.1 Frequently concealed -ISMS

Scepticism and education

Most people can appreciate that scepticism, applied with discretion, is important as a safeguard against credulity and straight conditioning. The word 'critical' is however more apposite because it does not imply a settled conviction. Furthermore the negative ring of 'scepticism' is unhelpful.

With regard to scepticism, people are seeing that non-provable values are unavoidable and a necessary aspect of being a person. The case for acknowledging that all schooling is value-laden, and all teachers act from commitment to certain values, needs to be argued much less today than was necessary in educational circles even a decade ago.

Particular values cannot be doubted without resting upon other values which are not doubted. Doubting is only a part, and often not the most important part, of education in its ideal sense, for 'respect' has as much or more to do with affirmation. Yet frequently the impression given in schools, colleges and universities is that the ability to doubt is the highest academic achievement. Subjects such as history have been frequently proclaimed as a training in doubt. Respect does not preclude criticism, but it cannot survive in an atmosphere of radical doubt.

Reductionism and education

Allied to confidence in scientific method, and so-called objective statistical analysis, scepticism of some aspects of life reinforces the reductionism which is so important a feature of much schooling. This therefore calls for more detailed comment. Reductionism points to the need to isolate factors in order to arrive at factual knowledge. Such isolation is unavoidable. We cannot attend to everything all the time. It is important to recognise what we are doing, however – that in concentrating on this we are marginalising something else. And we have to make allowances for this whenever we make generalisations which are unavoidable if we try to communicate at all.

Nearly two centuries ago, Coleridge struggled to help people to see this (Note 4, p. 53). He drew attention to the difference between distinguishing and separating, as e.g. the hand from the body.

To analyse, clarify and distinguish one thing from another – in the interests of which, factors have to be isolated – is part of the process of learning to understand. This part should never, however, masquerade as the whole. The links between disciplines are as important as, or more important than, the distinctions, because reality itself is not neatly partitioned into separate compartments.

Reductionism is often the unintentional result of enthusiasm channelled in one direction and of specialist knowledge (see p.78 of Chapter 6). It is perpetuated however by the closed mind, which fails to distinguish between different kinds of evidence and 'reduces' them all to one kind. Reductionism in biology, for example, may 'reduce' human beings to the level of molecular machines, ignoring the data associated with consciousness. Reductionism in history may see a historical event as entirely due to economic and political causes, failing to consider, for example, the influence of ideas and of leading personalities, of sociological factors, or of the part played by the arts or by religion.

A particularly clear example of reductionism is Nietzsche's comment, 'Man is what he eats'. As a strong statement of the importance of the physical aspect of life this may have its place, but when taken as a complete statement it is misleading. It implies that nothing beyond the physical matters or exists. It is helpful to contrast this with the biblical saying, 'Man shall not live by bread alone'. This includes the importance of the physical within a much wider framework and is therefore not reductionist. This example relates directly to the prevalence of materialist, consumerist and competitive attitudes in schools, to which Tim Brighouse drew attention (see p.15 of Chapter 2).

Reductionism also shows itself in the compartmentalism of knowledge which is reinforced many times over by the way in which schooling is organised, especially at secondary and tertiary levels. Specialist teachers, timetabled slots and distinctive examination structures convey very effectively to students that learning does not – and need not – relate across subject areas.

There are fewer signs of reductionism being widely discredited as yet, probably because of the strength of conditioning resulting from years of compulsory and voluntary higher education.

Relativism and education

Another of the -isms which is becoming more widely challenged today is relativism. Some of the insights of relativism are shown in Figure 4.2.

Relativism underlines the importance of context in the development of people and the views they hold. As such it contains valuable insight. Yet it does so at a price – the price of not taking seriously the search for truth. This is another of the fundamental assumptions necessary to proceed with education.

Truth-claims are frequently ignored in education at every level. Attention is constantly drawn to what people say or believe, but the validity of what is thought is given little attention except where scientific method is appropriate. This is especially serious with regard to controversial issues, many of which are extremely important in considering all five aspects of the attitude of respect basic to education.

Typical of advice given to teachers on how to handle controversial subjects in class, is the following:

> It can be very helpful for pupils to know their teachers' views, providing these are offered as one among many possible perspectives on an issue with no more weight or 'truth' than any other. (Note 5, p. 53)

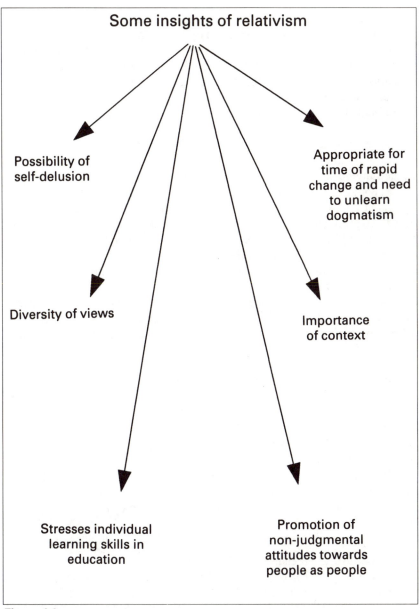

Figure 4.2

It is probable that the inspectors wrote this (and underlined the key phrase) against a background of situations where teachers used their authority in such a way that students would not take account of other divergent views. If, however, *this* kind of context for the advice is forgotten, or not appreciated, their words may easily be interpreted as appealing to the view that no-one *can* know and that degrees of significance need not be attached to statements.

This relativist assumption is extremely pervasive and subtly damaging to education; it inhibits any in-depth discussion of the values necessary to education by assuming from the start that they are subjective and just a matter of exploring a possible consensus. The underlying questions of the validity of values such as 'that people matter' are shelved on the vague assumption that human nature is basically amenable to reason, so it is quite safe to let people choose their values.

Yet one can imagine a young Hitler undergoing such a course in values education and receiving little to make him think further than this: 'Why do other people matter if I can ensure that their disapproval doesn't damage me? That is, if I am stronger than them? And *why* shouldn't this society fall apart if I can create a better one in which I am boss and do what I like? And if I can set this up by using the weakness, vagueness and illogicality of the "nice" people in my present society, so be it. Their sense of the importance of being fair to me will be my ladder to the success of my own intentions; and when I've got where I want I can kick them away.'

Discussion or teaching based on relativism is dangerous in its naivety. Schools must look deeper; they must, in fact, challenge the assumption. If everything is relative, and any opinion is as good as another regardless of considerations of evidence, logical consistency, comprehensiveness, or experience, then the basis for civilisation is destroyed. What will inevitably happen is that the one who shouts loudest and longest will prevail.

Nature abhors a vacuum. Action and lifestyle depend upon underlying values, principles, or convictions, strong or weak, acknowledged or not acknowledged, known or hidden, chosen or conditioned. If people do not think these out properly for themselves, they will be swept along by whatever is most forceful in their environment.

It is important to appreciate what is at stake here. Talk of choice is appropriate in that education concerns the development of people's capacity for freedom and informed choice. Furthermore choice aids commitment if made authentically.

The problem with relativism is well expressed in the following quotation:

> How can all truth be relative? For is it only 'relatively true' that 'truth is relative'? If so, relativism itself is simply 'one way of looking at things' and it tells us nothing at all. From another language, another perspective, truth may not be relative. The relativist view makes stronger claims. It is not just that, from one perspective, truth is relative, but . . . truth is relative – from all perspectives, for all languages. In other words, according to relativism, it is an absolute truth that all truth is relative. We have arrived at the famous – and inescapable – paradox of relativism. The statement of the view contradicts itself in the very act of being stated. If it is true then it is false. (Note 6, p.53)

When we reach such an absurd situation we are entitled to ask whether

Figure 4.3 The collapse of earlier certainties or -ISMS has encouraged the flowering of others

something is wrong with the initial premises. Figure 4.3 points to three responses to this situation, one of which is especially important and novel, and we shall devote the rest of the chapter to this. The undermining of former -isms has produced this interesting new phenomenon.

Postmodernism

There can be a fifth possible response to the proposition on p. 41 concerning the moral law: 'Yes, there is no such *moral* law because such terms imply the existence of true standards, but truth is a concept which it is no longer possible to retain. There can be no sustainable theory. *Anti-social* can act as a perfectly adequate principle for action in our post-truth situation.' (Postmodernism)

The use of the term 'postmodernism' has greatly increased in the last few years. Originating in the 1960s, it has been applied to a wide variety of situations. There is much debate as to what exactly is meant by it. It is probably fair to say that it indicates above all a mood of disenchantment with metaphysics in any shape or form, and a pragmatic determination to get on with life in as liberated, efficient and enjoyable a way as possible.

Basically the postmodernist says we must operate at a post-theory level – past attempting to give any meaning to things as a whole. Every theory is untenable, and there is no point in trying to adjudicate between them, except in order to find what suits a person best. There is and can be no objectivity in truth, and it is best to give up any attempt to find it. They note, 'We must learn to live after truth', as one Postmodernist Manifesto puts it (Note 6, p.53). It goes on:

> Our story begins with a crisis. Our most sacred values, our most certain judgements, our most solid truths have lost their value, their certainty, their truth. We can neither live with them nor without them. We have nothing left to cling on to. Religion, humanism, science are all thrown into doubt. We face a crisis of nihilism . . . in two stages: relativism and reflexivity. When we consider the status of our theories and our truth we are led to relativism. Relativism, in turn, turns back on itself and disappears into the vicious spiral of reflexivity. 'Nothing is certain, not even this.'

The conclusion they draw from this is that:

> . . . . there are many 'truths' . . . They are not truths which set out to tell us what is the case, to correspond to a pre-given reality. It is not as if they could be 'falsified' and replaced by the 'real' truth. They are, in this sense, fictions, fictions that guide our behaviour, fictions in a world where there is no non-fiction, where there is no fact. Truths are the stories through which we have our worlds and ourselves . . . like the furniture in a room. They may no longer fit, we may want different shapes or different functions – they can even wear out with over-use . . . . What matters is not that these truths, these stories, match some reality, but that they work, that they serve their purpose (pp. 22–3). (Note 6, p. 53)

Page 30 of the Manifesto continues:

> In this process the world will regain its mystery which, under rationalism, it has lost. For rationalism set out to demystify the world and has ended up unmasking itself. There is nowhere else to start from but where we are.

And the booklet finishes with these words:

> A postmodern manifesto is a performance, a call to action. The rationalists have only interpreted the world, the point is to invent it! (p.31)

There is much that is exhilarating here. The message is, create your own stories, write your own life narratives. It's all up to you, and no one is in a position to say yea or nay unless you choose to play that game. This can be very liberating to people who have become imprisoned within outworn beliefs and forms of words – ill-understood and narrow in implication – and for whom it is essential to adopt a fresh perspective. Postmodernism invites people to do just that.

Just as with the other -isms, there is a lot that is positive about postmodernism. Reason and/or science have been mistakenly put on a pedestal so that everything has to be judged by them – rather like assuming that everything must be judged by its taste and disclaiming knowledge which might reach us via other senses, for instance by hearing. It is important that this pedestal be toppled. There is no reason why we should limit ourselves to crawling along the ground when we could be flying, especially when we come to water to be crossed!

Unfortunately the perspective it offers is itself deeply flawed, at both logical and existential levels. Logically, the problem is that postmodernism too is theory, and it *could* be wrong. If it is wrong, the postmodernist assurances that there is no such thing as right and wrong will simply be like seaweed left on the shore as the tide goes out.

To maintain that there is no theory can be seen existentially as well as logically to fail. People – including the postmodernists – again and again act as though there were! Not of course if theory is understood as an official creed, but increasingly it is perceived that basic assumptions are operating all the time in people's lives, and do generate how they behave and respond, how they act and react.

Postmodernism does not escape the circles because it is in effect a backlash from the assumption which it denies. It does not offer a revision of that assumption which is substantial on its own. Postmodernism is therefore essentially parasitical, dependent on the climate whose existence it denies. It can therefore readily collapse into the lifestyle created by the organism it denies.

Postmodernism is a shaky platform *per se.* Its value above all is in drawing attention to the failures of rationalism and in its introducing into metaphysics metaphors of fluidity rather than of something static.

TASK 4.1

Study Figure 4.1

1. What do you notice about how these -isms are arranged?
2. Can you add to the list in either circle?
3. Is there something right about all or most of these -isms? Go through each, identifying any insight they draw attention to.
4. Is there something wrong about all or most of them?

TASK 4.2

Relate these comments to the different -isms:

1. 'You should always doubt if you can.'
2. 'Man is what he eats.'
3. 'I'm all right, Jack.'
4. 'The very latest video – you can't do without it.'

5. 'Don't sit there doing nothing.'
6. 'Well, that's just your view; someone else from a different background would argue something different.'
7. 'Forget about truth – you can argue about that till kingdom come!'
8. 'If you can't prove it scientifically, it's not fact, just somebody's opinion.'
9. 'What really matters is the physical world and that we need to exploit it.'

TASK 4.3

ICONS FOR -ISMS
Devise icons to indicate the
-isms listed in FIGURE 4.1.
Here are a few suggestions:

POSITIVISM

SCEPTICISM

? ?????????????,,,,

REDUCTIONISM

TASK 4.4

Write the -ism below each one of these statements:

I am what culture has made me
_____

I am what I do
_____

I am what I have
_____

I am the simplest, most basic ingredient
_____

??????????
?WHO AM I?
??????????

I am my body
_____

I am what I think and doubt
_____

I am what I create
_____

I am what science describes
_____

I am what I choose
_____

TASK 4.5

Which -isms are represented by these different comments about the cat?

1. Sentimental attachment to pets is

3. Folk say that keeping a cat helps old people live longer – but there's no proof.

2. I love the freedom of a cat's movements – it's a real inspiration.

4. The snag is a cat makes more housework – its hairs get everywhere.

8. Guess it's not worth much.

5. The cat is a member of the feline family. Its domestication is well-attested in fossils and

6. The cat is a loner – just like people should be – doing their own

7. Wouldn't have a cat – can't go for walks with it.

TASK 4.6

List all the National Curriculum subjects in order of importance for:

1. an activist,

2. a sceptic,

3. a relativist,

4. a materialist,

5. a positivist,

6. a postmodernist.

Notes

1. Pring, R. (1987) *Personal, Social and Moral Education in a Changing World* edited by Thacker, Pring and Evans, NFER – Nelson, p.27.

2. 'Phronesis', See Aristotle: *The Nicomachean Ethics* 1104 A9; B23.

3. Ayer, A.J. (1940) *Language, Truth and Logic*, and (1940) *The Foundations of Empirical Knowledge*, Gollancz.

4. For Coleridge see Barfield, Owen (1971) *What Coleridge Thought*, Wesleyan University Press, pp. 18–21.

5. From *History and Social Sciences at Secondary Level Part III*, ILEA 1983, p.48.

6. The Second of January Group (April 1986) in their manifesto *After Truth: A Post-Modern Manifesto* (pps. 19f, 3, 22–3, 30, 31).

Chapter 5

Adjudicating Assumptions

We have unearthed some of the root assumptions at work today which are producing serious doubts about the status and validity of 'moral' values. Figure 5.1 shows how these -isms have robbed *moral* of any sense of universal applicability or of absolute non-negotiable obligation such that society itself is to be judged by *moral* standards rather than the other way round.

Different conclusions are drawn from this assumption. Some see the assumption as liberation – as an invitation to take hold of situations, kick over the traces of past subservience to the rules imposed, and learn to be creative. Others see 'morality' as the way in which those dominant within a society strive to stay in power by subjecting the rest to it. Still others – perhaps the majority – fear the vacuum thus created in which the values essential for civilised life become less certain because subject to the vagaries of people's imagination or will to power. They therefore recoil from the cognitive relativism involved in the assumption yet, because they do not challenge the underlying assumption itself, they endeavour to keep the ship afloat and accommodate their strong feelings for justice by using euphemisms for 'moral' such as 'socially-acceptable', 'positive', 'creative', 'beneficial', etc., as though all were agreed regarding the reference-points for these terms. We suspect that mostly they know that all are not agreed, but that they think that if they hurry over such phrases no one will notice!

These substitutes for 'moral', however, all beg the question: 'socially-acceptable' to whom? 'positive' in what sense? 'creative' for what? 'beneficial' for whom and in what way? It is hard to avoid the conclusion that these phrases are a cop-out. They purport to be straight-forward, literal, descriptive, non-'moral', value-free phrases, when they carry massive but unacknowledged imported, emotional content and unargued-for value-judgements.

We now turn to the challenge presented by C in the conversation at the beginning of Chapter 4. Concerning the assumptions that there *is* a moral law, or that there *is not* a moral law, C suggested that there is more evidence in favour of one of these assumptions than the other. Immediately, however, we are faced with two equally inappropriate possibilities:

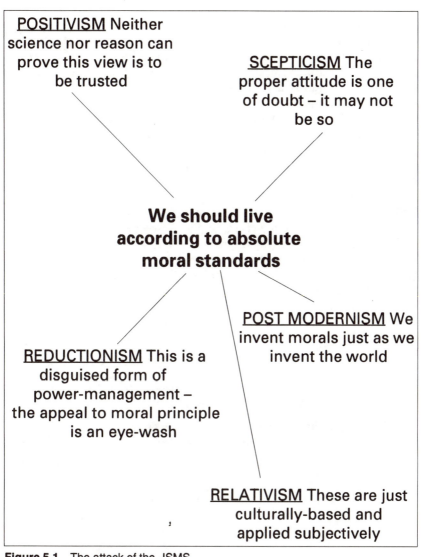

POSITIVISM Neither science nor reason can prove this view is to be trusted

SCEPTICISM The proper attitude is one of doubt – it may not be so

We should live according to absolute moral standards

POST MODERNISM We invent morals just as we invent the world

REDUCTIONISM This is a disguised form of power-management – the appeal to moral principle is an eye-wash

RELATIVISM These are just culturally-based and applied subjectively

Figure 5.1 The attack of the -ISMS

A. that there cannot be any *evidence* to put forward, and

B. that any appeal to evidence must constitute cast-iron *proof*.

A. Is there such a thing as evidence?

Many today, under the influence of the -isms, and especially postmodernism, argue that such an appeal to evidence is illusory. There are *no* grounds, except

56

purely self-chosen ones, for preferring one statement to another. Even within a culture, what one person calls evidence is discounted by another. No proof is available unless people have already agreed to play the game, and abide by the rules chosen. But such rules vary from culture to culture, sub-culture to sub-culture, and individual to individual. The goal-posts are constantly changing.

Even if there *are* trans-cultural criteria – i.e. similar criteria found independently within different cultures – such can be regarded as just part of a new culture which is 'trans-the-old-culture', and this is still to be playing the culture game: no relationship to truth can be claimed between what we say and truth itself.

What constitutes evidence is as unagreed as the content of what is being discussed. For evidence too is interpreted subjectively, like the person who denies the existence of albino crows, and when someone points one out, s/he simply denies that this particular bird is a crow!

There can be arguments about the process of how we decide, the scaffolding, the picture-frame, the meta-categories, as well as on the content of what we are deciding about. Furthermore, acceptance of particular evidence as evidence rests on principles or values brought to the discussion rather than rising from it. There is a chicken-or-egg situation concerning all talk of values and criteria discussion. As one philosopher has put it:

> Values, of course, influence to some extent the selection by a philosopher of the guiding principles of his reflection. Indeed, the final cause always orientates the agent cause. But the principles themselves may very well determine the kind of values which the philosopher's reflection will finally ascertain. (Note 1, p. 69)

Therefore why bother to waste time and energy on truth questions under the illusion that we can ever reach any certainty that way?

This presumed absence of any trans-cultural, trans-subjective criteria is however open to being discredited on a number of grounds:

1. If it is an appropriate assumption, there is no way that any evidence can support its being so. If nothing is or can be true, then the postmodernist is not in a position to say so, for of course nothing s/he says can be true either. The branch of the tree on which we all sit has been sawn off and that's the end of the matter.

2. Such an attitude to the question of evidence has to ignore a vast amount of human experience and knowledge. Most areas of life which we care about: the sciences, humanities, arts, politics, morals, etc. become sheer idle pleasantries rather than matter for intelligent debate if no appeal to evidence of any kind is possible, or to be allowed.

   To leave out of consideration altogether the possibility of knowledge concerning such aspects of life is a sign of inadequacy.

3. In everyday living we are constantly being forced to recognise the validity of sheer factual evidence whether we like it or not, especially when it is hard

to find out the truth of a situation. If, for example, there are different reports about whether a water-supply is contaminated or not, it matters very much that we find out whether it actually is: evidence has to be weighed.

4. Existentially, we all know from our experience – from what it feels like to be human – that we ourselves transcend such factual matters and yet that we do consider evidence. Someone who has fallen in love will look anxiously for tell-tale signs of love being reciprocated. The evidence is rarely straight-forwardly factual but it can make a profound difference to the success or otherwise of the relationship.

5. A particularly strong argument for trans-cultural criteria consists in the fact that cultures very different from Western traditions use criteria which closely resemble those found within Western traditions. In India, for example, the various schools of philosophy, especially the *Mimamsa* school, distinguish in closely rational manner between different ways of knowing (*pramanas*). These have recognisable equivalents in the West (Note 2, p.69).

Criteria common to Indian and Western thought

This is so important a consideration that it is worth developing rather more fully. Richard de Smet, long resident in India, has argued that three basic principles underlie most Indian reflection:

(i) Viveka – a principle of analysing and discriminating between what is presented. De Smet quotes one of the greatest Indian thinkers, Sankara:

> As the flamingo sifts milk from the water, so the wise man sifts the excellent from the mere pleasant, going mentally all around these two objects, examining them closely, weighing their respective importance or futility; and having distinguished them, he chooses the excellent alone on account of its superiority. (Note 3, p.69)

Like philosophers in the West, they distinguished subject from object, cause from effects, and spiritual values from those just relating to the enjoyment of the senses. De Smet considers that they went further indeed and tended to isolate the essential from the dependent, the unchanging from the changing, and finally refused to apply such terms as 'being', 'true', 'meaningful', or 'valuable' to anything but the permanent and even the absolutely permanent, the uncaused pure Consciousness (Note 3, p.69).

(ii) arthapatti – deduction.

De Smet gives the stock example of *arthapatti*:

> If observation assures me that my neighbour never eats during the daytime and yet keeps perfectly healthy and vigorous, I quite logically assume that he must be accustomed to eat during the night. More generally, when I am confronted with two

facts or statements which are well-ascertained by perception or any one of the other *pramanas* (valid sources of knowledge) and which, at the same time, appear to clash, I am logically allowed to look for an unperceived condition which will suffice to reconcile those opposed facts. The subsidiary principle of economy will then guide me in selecting, among the many possible sufficient conditions, that one which is most simple and most conforming to the ordinary course of existence. The probability that this is the real explanation of the case will then approach a practical certainty. (Note 3, p. 69)

This principle is used by scientists, by detectives trying to solve a crime, by historians trying to understand the past, and by everyone in everyday life as they work out reasons for apparently contradictory phenomena.

(iii) laksana – analogy.

This principle acknowledges the way in which words can have a secondary meaning which fit them to say something concerning different situations because something similar can be seen. Language develops in this way. De Smet gives a typical example from Indian thought:

> In the sentence, 'Look at that hamlet on the Ganga', the preposition 'on' loses its proper meaning, which is 'on the surface of', and its association with 'hamlet' and 'Ganga' forces it to don the analogical meaning of 'along' or 'on the bank of'. . . . (in this way) words which originally had just a physical reference can become appropriate vehicles for spiritual concepts and ideals. (Note 3, p. 69)

This use of language is clearly related to the role of *metaphor* in the West, the importance of which in philosophy is increasingly acknowledged today (Note 4, p. 69).

In addition to these three principles, De Smet argues that another standard Indian way of arguing – the process known as *khandana*, meaning refutation – is in fact also found in the West (Note 5, p. 69). It refers to the importance of avoiding absurdities in arguing, adding significantly that failure to address difficulties in an argument amounts to losing the case. Such failure to address an objection is itself a sign of the inadequacy of a position. To marginalise an argument is in effect to concede defeat. If members of a committee, for example, fail to articulate an objection, they must be considered unable to answer it.

Another criterion well-attested within Indian philosophy is that of competent authority: the traditions, written and oral, associated with revered sages and seers have the status of *sabda* – authentic witness. In the West, unavoidable dependence upon specialists is also acknowledged as necessary because it is impossible to devote the time, energy, and skill necessary to discovering everything oneself. So a proper test of an assumption could be: does it have the support of major traditions, or of people who have devoted responsible attention to it?

This approach to knowledge does not dismiss reasoning, but simply acknowledges its insufficiency by itself. For reason can only give us opinion, not

unchallengable certainty, but life and knowledge require and display conviction.

Criteria which are not just culture-bound

To summarise this section, we can list at least the following principles as
trans-cultural:

- Logical coherence and consistency – whereby different aspects fit together
  and can relate logically without contradiction (*viveka*).

- Explanatory power – that which helps people make sense of experience
  (*arthapatti*). In the form of a question: Does an assumption offer an
  adequate explanation for some aspect of life, event, or experience?

- Openness and the capacity to be creative in perceiving links between aspects
  of life with the possibility of receiving fresh insight (*laksana*). We can ask
  of an assumption: Is it welcoming to fresh experience, or is it dogmatically
  narrow?

- Comprehensive – that nothing is excluded which is important and which
  ought to be represented – that to fail to address certain areas of experience
  is tantamount to inability to include them (*khandana*). This principle relates
  to the degree to which an assumption can potentially take on board, in
  ever-widening circles, all experience and facts encountered. Does the assumption indeed promote a unified view of life, or is it exclusivist, parochial
  or one-sided?

- Competent authority – that we enter into a tradition and do not have to
  reinvent the wheel. Indeed we are dependent on the insight of others as well
  as our own (*sabda*).

- Another criteria would seem to be that of sustainability or chronic vigour
  – basically the test of time. Within Indian thought this notion is implied
  rather than stated because of the radically cyclic concept of reality with
  which they operate. The ceaseless movement of *samsara* – the sea of birth
  and re-birth – assumes sustainability and a quality of enduringness over the
  centuries. This principle invites the question: Is the assumption likely to be
  of only short duration, or is it likely to be sustainable over a long period of
  time and/or in many different circumstances?

All the above constitute publicly identifiable evidence that certain criteria
transcend culture, in the sense that they are used within cultures without any
concern at all for relating to other cultures. In other words, the same criteria
are appealed to inherently within different cultures. This must call into doubt
an assumption that there are no such criteria.

On the basis of these six criteria it is possible to posit a further one. That of
social responsibility. Associated with the other criteria listed, more meaningful

60

content can be given to the notion of social responsibility beyond what this person or that happens to think is socially beneficial. It signifies that which builds up social life, encouraging socially acceptable behaviour. This includes acknowledging the rights of others as well as oneself, and being capable of acting fairly and reciprocally on the basis of empathy.

None of these criteria exempts us from the difficult task of interpreting and applying them appropriately (cf. the *phronesis* of Aristotle). If criteria are indeed thought of as static rules just waiting to be applied mechanically then we can agree that none such exist! But criteria should not be seen in this light (see discussion on p. 63 of the value of metaphors suggesting fluidity). Rather, criteria are not proofs but considerations to be applied to concrete situations.

If the criteria are accepted, points of reference are established. If people refuse to accept them, then it should be made clear that unless they can establish other valid criteria, meaningful discussion is at an end.

B. Evidence must be proof

This heading suggests that there must be no room for doubt. Evidence must give absolute certainty. It is important, however, not to go to the other extreme. If the idea of evidence is reinstated it can easily be expected to constitute *proof* – to be unchallengeable and available for all with the intelligence and training necessary to see it. Cognitively speaking, underlying this attitude is a desire for absolute certainty which is assumed to be possible. Because of the enormous temptation to try to find cast-iron proof, the limitations of reasoning need constantly to be borne in mind. Reason can only be an aid, and not the final unassailable arbiter which some of its advocates wish it to be.

Perhaps the analogy of travel may help to clarify the role of reason. If we are going on a journey, it is not reason but empirical facticity that decides the starting-point: we cannot set off from where we are not! Even when on our way, we may have to trust a hunch rather than rely on carefully-worked-out map-reading regarding the route. *Considerations* are more fundamental than *proofs*. The validity of the latter with regard to the real world depends on the former, whilst proofs cannot demolish considerations.

Reason comes into its own in showing up specious or dishonest thinking. It can knock down, for example, a case where someone is given a job after an interview 'because s/he's had such a traumatic time' as a dishonest way of reasoning – a fallacy in which an attempt to establish fact (suitability for the job) – is made from an appeal for pity *ad misericordiam*. But it cannot prove that pity is not a consideration alongside others, and maybe one which should in certain circumstances take precedence over them on other grounds.

The search for certainty is understandable and legitimate in that it seeks to guard against illusion. If focussed on too long and too intently, however, it can get hi-jacked into becoming an obsession. In this sense it represents a desire to escape from the unending and difficult but unavoidable balancing and weighing of evidence in the ongoingness of life, and the need for constant responsible monitoring of what we are certain about and why.

Dependence of the -isms on a search for absolute certainty

The search for absolute certainty is fundamentally the power-house behind these -isms (see Figure 5.2). This assumption promotes on the one hand a cult

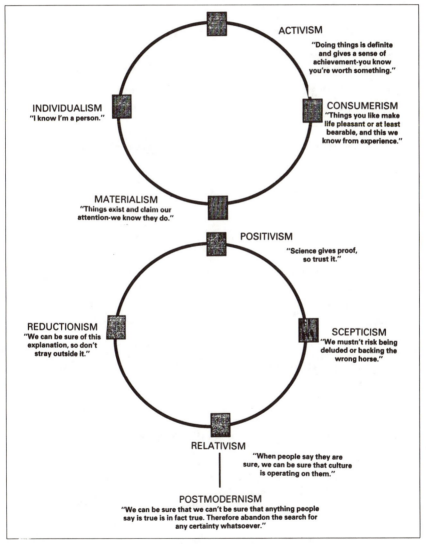

ACTIVISM
"Doing things is definite and gives a sense of achievement-you know you're worth something."

CONSUMERISM
"Things you like make life pleasant or at least bearable, and this we know from experience."

INDIVIDUALISM
"I know I'm a person."

MATERIALISM
"Things exist and claim our attention-we know they do."

POSITIVISM
"Science gives proof, so trust it."

REDUCTIONISM
"We can be sure of this explanation, so don't stray outside it."

SCEPTICISM
"We mustn't risk being deluded or backing the wrong horse."

RELATIVISM
"When people say they are sure, we can be sure that culture is operating on them."

POSTMODERNISM
"We can be sure that we can't be sure that anything people say is true is in fact true. Therefore abandon the search for any certainty whatsoever."

Figure 5.2 On being absolutely sure

62

of objectivity, literalism, and the use of reason and scientific method, and on the other a corresponding suspicion of subjectivity, of the metaphorical, and of the arts (see Figure 5.3 which also gives possible reasons for challenging the assumption).

It is to be noted that postmodernism is dependent, though subtly, on this assumption of the possibility of absolute certainty. Postmodernism is a phenomenon which has arisen in reaction to the operation of particular assumptions all associated and powered by this assumption.

Applying the seven criteria given on p. 59 to the view that such provable certainty is possible produces a clearly negative result. Task 5.1 sets this out

FALSE EITHER / OR

L.H. SIDE OF THE BRAIN	R.H. SIDE OF THE BRAIN
CULT OF **OBJECTIVITY**	SUSPICION OF **SUBJECTIVITY**
CULT OF **THE LITERAL**	SUSPICION OF THE **METAPHORICAL**
CULT OF THE **RATIONAL/SCIENTIFIC**	SUSPICION OF **THE ARTS**

WHY THIS IS MISTAKEN:

*BILLIONS OF FACTORS OPERATING ALL THE TIME - IMPOSSIBLE TO KNOW THEM ALL - IMPRESSIVE SCIENTIFIC EVIDENCE HAS ADDED WEIGHT TO WHAT CAN BE INTUITED FROM THE SIMPLEST EVERYDAY EXPERIENCE AND REFLECTION e.g. LORENZ'S "BUTTERFLY EFFECT".

*THE CONSTANT ON-GOINGNESS AND CHANGE OF LIFE. NOTHING REMAINS THE SAME. ALL IS IN PROCESS OF CREATION, DISINTEGRATION OR TRANSFORMATION. e.g. MODERN QUANTUM PHYSICS.

*THE FINITUDE OF HUMAN EXPERIENCE AND INTELLECTUAL CAPACITY. EVEN THE CLEVEREST CAN ONLY KNOW A FRACTION OF WHAT IS TO BE KNOWN e.g. SOCRATES, NEWTON, EINSTEIN.

*THE EXPERIENCE OF PERSONAL CONSCIOUSNESS OF LIVING BY WHAT WE KNOW, YET KNOWING ALSO DEEP-DOWN THAT THE POSSIBILITY OF DELUSION, IGNORANCE, PARTIALITY, MISUNDERSTANDING, BIAS ETC. THREATENS ALL WE KNOW.

Figure 5.3

in a form which could be used as a template for testing other assumptions. Readers might like to try this out with regard to some other view which they feel strongly about but which is frequently consigned to the category of 'just opinion'.

What metaphor shall we use for knowledge?

The evidence is overwhelming that we cannot have such absolutely secure, water-tight certainty – not, at least, on matters of the most trivial and mundane nature, for example that human beings normally have ten toes! The vast majority of important matters on which decisions have to be made, which include the most particular every-day usage of time, energy and money as well as the profound issues of life and death, *cannot* plug into unassailably reliable authoritative reservoirs of knowledge. The postmodernist is right about this! Attempts at proof simply do not hold water.

A metaphor alluded to three times in the last paragraph – that of water – indicates the difficulty of control regarding knowledge. Knowledge remains obdurately fluid not static. Yet a static mode of thinking is constantly reinforced by the -isms which meet us in so many walks of life.

1. The over-emphasis on science and technological achievement and the undervaluing of, for example, the arts which would and should counterbalance it (Positivism).

2. The over-emphasis on criticism and looking for faults rather than noticing what is right. Cf. the impact of the media, in which what is controversial, wayward, unfortunate, or evil tends to take centre stage (Scepticism).

3. The shutting-off of certain perspectives as illegitimate, so that many people do not even know there is another way of looking at things, for example, the artistic perspective; and even if they do, they easily feel guilty or ill at ease in exploring another perspective, on the grounds that it is hopelessly subjective (Reductionism).

4. The constant undermining of certain views which do not conform to the above emphases by the implication: 'That's only *your* opinion', thus diminishing the question of evidence and discouraging people from much serious reflection, because 'it can only be my opinion anyway' (Relativism).

5. The prevalence of a pragmatic attitude which says: 'Don't bother your head about all these intellectual matters. Just get on with the business of living.' In a world of economic, political and cultural change, people lurch forward, happily or otherwise, without any guiding ropes apart from those which happen to be inbuilt (which largely they do not know about or acknowledge), and the events which chance to happen (Postmodernism).

We have been seriously misled by the static types of metaphor generated, especially in discussion of education. Facts to be memorised, stages of development to be marked, age-groups put into classrooms, timetable slots in which subjects are to be learned, achievements to be assessed, syllabuses to be studied, subject areas as compartments into which knowledge is clearly divided. The hidden but real impact of the constant use of such a framework in our thinking about knowledge and learning is to reinforce the fence-mentality: 'We can be sure of this if we put a barrier round it.'

A different starting-point?

We need to expose the illegitimate certainty of the underlying assumption behind these -isms, namely that we *can* have such certainty. Attempts to attain such unchallengeable certainty result either in reducing the field of enquiry to one which we think of as amenable, as in science – even though science itself cannot be so contained, as twentieth century discoveries have shown – or in pretending that we are certain when we are not – self-deception in fact.

We need a different assumption to which we then apply the criteria discussed above (p. 59). We need one which:

- is logically coherent so that it is not self-contradictory;

- makes a real attempt to offer adequate explanation of phenomena encountered;

- allows for openness in the on-going task of reaching towards truth;

- is potentially all-embracing and not exclusive;

- relates constructively to traditions;

- really is sustainable on its own;

- promotes healthy co-operation.

This is provided for in the following assumption: that reliable certainty is possible which is partial and provisional. If we apply these criteria to this proposition we come up with a very positive assessment (see Figure 5.4).

This assumption takes on board the undoubted fact that people consistently display certainty, and have to in order to live at all, think at all, act at all. It allows, however, for that essential element of 'ongoingness', fluidity and need for some change as fresh experiences come our way. Such certainty is justified but not in any absolute fashion. People can trust their certainty justifiably to the extent that they acknowledge that what they know is limited – is partial, and therefore open to wider and deeper interpretation and forms of expression as more experience conveys more insight. The certainty is therefore provisional in that sense.

This indeed invites exploration, and encourages a positive attitude to the experience of others as well as of oneself. It therefore takes on board fully those anxieties to avoid narrow dogmatism which are felt especially by most pro-

RELIABLE CERTAINTY WHICH IS PARTIAL AND PROVISIONAL IS POSSIBLE

1. that it is not contradictory, not
   requiring proof in order to be true

2. that it holds the possibility of an
   adequate explanation at all levels

3. that it is welcoming to fresh insight

4. that it is comprehensive,

5. that most traditions support it,

6. that it sustains life, that
   people actually live on this basis

7. that it is affirming of people and
   permits good relationships,
   personal stability
   and an ongoing
   search for truth

Figure 5.4 Testing an assumption

ponents of relativism and postmodernism. Being dogmatic about the tiny fraction of knowledge which in fact is possible for any of us is indeed laughable. Even within a framework of co-operation with others, the case for intellectual arrogance remains impressively meagre.

This assumption, therefore, that we can have certainty but that it is necessarily partial and provisional, nourishes instead of jeopardising the search for knowledge, yet it does so in a way which can help to ensure a proper modesty and humility.

In the end we have to choose between these assumptions. We cannot adhere to both. *Absolute* certainty is not *partial and provisional* certainty. The advantages of the latter assumption are profound. Besides its being actually viable, it releases us from the neurotic search for such precise definiteness that we remain blind to so many other aspects of experience which otherwise would be obvious to us. It can help to save us from a dangerous either/or attitude.

Finally – two chapters later! – we come back to the challenge posed by C in the conversation that opened Chapter 4. The impact of the -isms on the notion

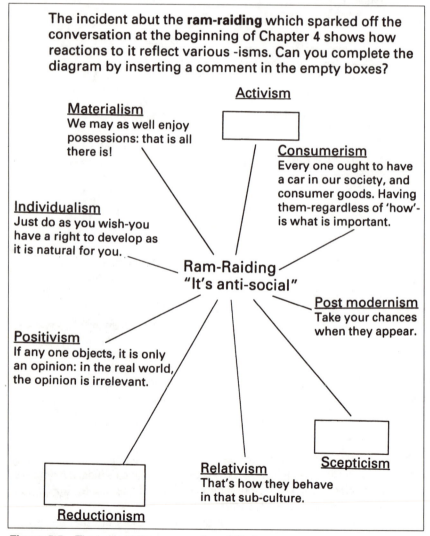

Figure 5.5 The ram-raiding comment re-visited

of the moral law was suggested in Figure 5.1. Figure 5.5 relates the -isms to the comment about ram-raiding. But these -isms themselves rest on evidence which can be discredited. This carries the corollary of throwing into doubt the

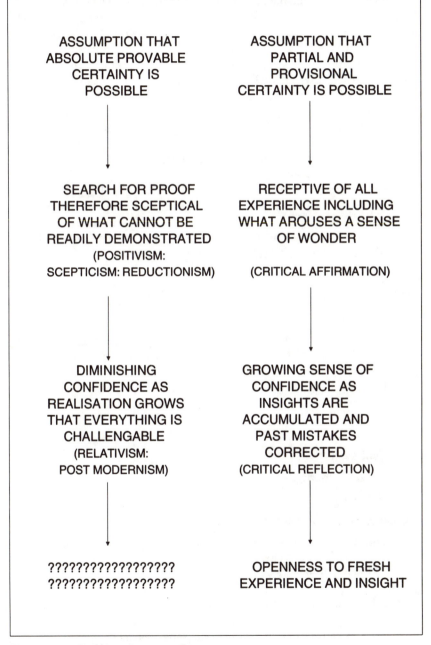

Figure 5.6 Choice and consequences

assumption based on those foundations concerning the non-existence of any moral law. Figure 5.6 sets out one possible way of assessing causes and effects over this.

It may help to clothe the abstract nature of these two last chapters with a little pictorial covering. The -isms may be likened to armed bandits who conspire to kidnap Conscience. She stands for that deep sense of justice which is probably present in almost everyone. The -isms support each other and successfully capture Conscience. They then brainwash her into confessing her own non-existence! What we have tried to do in this book is to liberate her from their clutches. In so doing, however, we are mindful that this is but the beginning of another story – another potential hazard to be guarded against. For Conscience traditionally has been subject to defilement from a quite different quarter, that of the chronic self-centredness and self-opinionatedness of people. Instead of opposing Conscience openly, this enemy has ever been set on taking her over with specious arguments. In this way Conscience herself has become warped and even sometime a cloak for naked self-aggrandisement.

What we are arguing for is a proper vigilance using reason and all other criteria available to try to guard against such an assault. The following chapter attempts to put in place a line of defence against serious mis-use of their responsibilities by such natural guardians of Conscience.

TASK 5.1 ASSUMPTION TO BE TESTED:

'Absolute certainty is possible if provable'

There are various tests which can be applied to an assumption such as the one above. Sort out which of the following considerations embodies which criteria and arrange them under the headings given:

1. **Logical coherence**

2. **Explanatory power**

3. **Openness**

4. **Comprehensiveness**

5. **Competent authority**

6. **Sustainability**

7. **Creative and beneficial consequences**

(a) It is not comprehensive because it leaves out of consideration huge areas of human experience and interest which are not amenable to cast-iron proof. This now includes science itself.

(b) This assumption is not consistent with itself in that, if it is true, then it is not itself true. It cannot claim the status of knowledge because it itself lacks proof.

(c) This assumption cannot provide adequate explanations, even of natural phenomena, because it rules out imagination, sensitivity, model-making etc.

(d) This assumption produces doubt, negativity, distress, failure to engage with as much of the evidence as possible.

(e) Authority for accepting such an assumption rests with a few scientists and philosophers whose views have been seriously challenged (e.g. A.J. Ayer). The majority of the world's great traditions would not lend their support.

(f) This is a dogmatic statement allowing no room for any alternative or ongoing exploration.

(g) Such reliance of proof has long been advocated, but never practised, except selectively. Enlightened rationalism and positivism are relatively recent developments by comparison with other views of knowledge, and they have not yet shown themselves to be sustainable.

Notes

1. DeSmet, Richard in an article in *Philosophy Today* on 'Some Governing Principles in Indian Philosophy'. (The authors were sent a photocopy of this article, with no date supplied)
2. The Mimamsa school had six *pramanas*: *pratyaksa* – perception; *anumana* – inference; *upamana* – analogy; *sabda* – testimony; *arthapatti* – intuitive presumption; *anapalabdhi* – abstraction.
3. DeSmet, Ibid.
4. Ortony, A. (ed) (1979) *Metaphor and Thought*, Cambridge University Press.
5. DeSmet cites the case of Gilbert Ryle.

Chapter 6

A Positive Approach to Controversy

Controversy is part of life. A creative approach to it should be the birthright of every child. Schools have a special role to play here, and need to bear in mind the words of Charles Peguy: 'The greatest treachery is to steal away.' (Note 1, p. 84). Yet those more concerned with the alternative ways of bringing up children and young people which were discussed in Chapter 3 (nurture, the 'commodities' approach, or indoctrination) may easily bypass the need to help students cope with controversy. A single view on controversial issues can be conveyed so much more efficiently than by muddying the waters with question marks.

Even genuine educationalists can evade the issue through capitulating to a relativist view of controversy:

> 'Openness' is the only virtue which all primary education for more than fifty years has dedicated itself to inculcating. Openness – and the relativism that makes it the only plausible stance in the face of various claims to truth and various ways of life and kinds of human beings – is the great insight of our times. The true believer is the real danger. The study of history and of culture teaches that all the world was made in the past; men always thought they were right, and that led to wars, persecutions, slavery, xenophobia, racism and chauvinism. The point is not to correct the mistakes and really be right; rather it is not to think you are right at all. (Note 2, p. 84)

Bloom was speaking of the American scene, but this kind of attitude has been powerfully at work in most Western societies, and has resulted in avoiding real involvement with many important issues in schools. Much teaching has succumbed to superficiality by being robbed of the controversial elements in education – elements which enable students to gain real understanding because they are a vital part of the subject-matter.

Certain recent developments are beginning to stir people to see the dangers in this evasive attitude. The anti-racist movement, for example, expects teachers to take a strong line to persuade, and, if necessary, to enforce anti-racism. Such persuasiveness and enforcement on the part of those in positions of authority can itself threaten education, and yet education which fails to take seriously such issues as racism is already denying itself. Those who believe in the five-fold attitude of respect for which we have argued as the basis of education (see pp. 22–24) realise only too vividly that there are many ways in which respect does not operate in our schools and in our society. Failure to point this out may, perhaps legitimately, be seen as connivance at their perpetuation. The need for reform in trying to correct injustice is insistent. Constant evasion of discussing controversial issues in the classroom and of arousing any sense of responsibility with regard to these issues is not conducive to real education.

Educationalists have so far been unable to provide clear and adequate answers to the very real problems involved. How can teachers help students and even young children to become discerning without over-influencing them? How can they ensure that experience in school demonstrates and promotes fairness for all people (including those who are difficult); impartiality to all views (including those whom they dislike), and a balanced perspective in evaluating complex questions and data?

Should teachers aim at neutrality?

The concept of procedural neutrality has been frequently invoked in the legitimate and necessary search for a means to guard against indoctrination. Clearly, there is a real danger where a person with a strong commitment is in a teaching situation. It is easy for the mis-directing enthusiast, or for the bigot who has authority, to control young minds in a way which restricts them and obliges them to conform.

To require teachers to be neutral does not, however, resolve this problem. The arguments against the neutral position are numerous. Before listing these, however, we should first note that there are situations in which it is helpful for teachers to withhold or hide what they personally think. If, for example, a class betrays a 'follow-the-teacher' mentality, or dislikes the trouble of thinking for themselves, then reserve on the part of the teacher may be called for. However, the stance of neutrality is often, perhaps mostly, professionally inappropriate.

1. R. F. Dearden has noted that the airing of 'ignorant alternatives or mere indisciplined assertiveness' will not improve understanding. Furthermore the teacher may confront such massive prejudice that s/he is the only source of possible divergence, that is, acknowledging that other views are possible. In such situations teachers are professionally obliged to contribute their own views (Note 3, p.84).

2. The attempt to suppress one's own convictions has a highly constraining effect on the quality of teaching. It is not educationally desirable for the teacher to suppress all facial expression, humour or signs of interest in the subject. Such teaching suffers from a fatal flaw: it is boring.

    Yet the slightest nuance can betray one's real standpoint. The following comment was made by someone who has spent over 20 years advising and inspecting schools:

If there be such a thing as neutral teaching, which I greatly doubt, it is quite marvellously dull. We shall not interest pupils or students by attempts at neutrality of approach. What is required of us is indeed that we display our assumptions, and that we make the implicit explicit, but also that we are fair and have professional integrity in our work. (Note 4, p. 84)

3. Neutrality is impossible. Selection of material, manner of presentation, the handling of questions and discussion and what is omitted deliberately or otherwise all reflect a viewpoint. It is dishonest and damaging education-ally to pretend that this is not so; the neutral stance itself rests on assump-tions and convictions which, if not expressed and openly acknowledged, may contribute to indoctrination.

This example draws attention to an odd trick about the nature of commitment. The illusion that we can maintain neutrality has been so effective partly because of a simple mistake, that of defining commitment in a narrow sense: as that which is made outwardly obvious by adherence to a set of propositions: 'I believe in the Bible . . . or Chairman Mao' or whatever; or which is demonstrated by special behaviour such as saluting the flag or entering a special building like a mosque or church, when believers stand up and allow themselves to be counted.

A more insidious danger, however, is that this obsession with obviously explicit forms of commitment easily hides the less obvious: the minute, mildly fluctuating, and hardly realised examples of commitment which everyone, without exception, has. One of the most important duties of education is to seek to lay bare, clarify and evaluate precisely these numerous convictions which affect how we live but which may be obscure to us unless critically examined.

Is openness possible?

As far back as 1955 M. V. C. Jeffreys summed up what was needed (Note 5, p. 84). 'The guarantee of freedom is not the teacher's neutrality but his or her respect for the integrity of the pupil's personality.' He considered it to be most important for teachers to give examples of 'how the possession of well-thought out ideas and convictions gives depth to personality'. Teachers must always remember, however, that 'it is more important that our pupils should think for themselves than that they should think as we do.'

Such an attitude on the part of the teacher requires a quality of openness. This is a word constantly in use today. It denotes an attitude in which people are not closed and restricted in their sympathies but instead are prepared to consider, without hasty judgement, many different and new possibilities.

By itself, however, openness can be a misused concept, referring to the practice of non-reflectiveness whereby a person refuses to think about any-thing, but simply receives any and every notion that comes along. Such a state of permanent openness would be one of indoctrination because the person concerned would accept the judgements of other people without reflecting upon them. Furthermore, evaluation and choosing are unavoidable when contradictions appear and when matters of great importance are discussed.

This 'pseudo openness' has become a stance in itself, but it suffers from the same handicap as procedural neutrality: it is impossible in practice. Nor is it desirable. Always to be an outsider, describing or finding out what other people think without participating in the conversation, trivialises the subject and inhibits the person. People are not being open to Humanism or to Islam if they are not prepared to consider the possibility of becoming Humanists or Muslims.

What is needed is a creative circle running between openness and conviction as a way of coming to terms with new ideas and expression, getting on the wavelength of people and establishing meaningful relationships (see Figure 6.1).

The value of a four-fold openness

Despite these problems, openness is still a helpful term to use provided it is seen as an attitude of mind, and not allowed to become a dogmatic stance. Openness, properly understood, has four components. These correspond in part to the five attitudes of respect outlined in Chapter 3 (see Figure 3.1).

1. Openness to fresh evidence as it presents itself with regard to the question of truth. The opposite of this is a closed mind which prefers not to take seriously the possibility of further data and more perceptive interpretation.

2. Openness to the experience of others, seeking to affirm their insights and so arrive at an ever more comprehensive interpretation of life. Lack of interest in what others believe and value, and a failure to weigh these carefully in a positive way, is the mark of an immature, selfish attitude to life which imagines that 'what I know is all I need to know.'

3. Openness to appreciating the real needs and situations of other people, for example, their sensibilities, their level of understanding, their need for self-affirmation, all of which cannot be met by any form of dogmatic approach which diminishes the other as a person.

4. Openness to critical assessment of the ease with which people, including oneself, can be self-deluded. This constitutes the safeguard par excellence against practising the wrong kind of openness.

Such openness is not easy to practice, but it 'opens' the way to a far richer and deeper mode of living (see Figure 6.2).

74

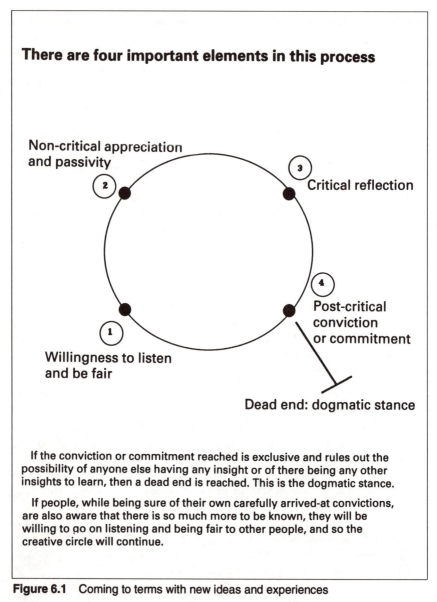

There are four important elements in this process

Non-critical appreciation and passivity

Critical reflection

Post-critical conviction or commitment

Willingness to listen and be fair

Dead end: dogmatic stance

If the conviction or commitment reached is exclusive and rules out the possibility of anyone else having any insight or of there being any other insights to learn, then a dead end is reached. This is the dogmatic stance.

If people, while being sure of their own carefully arrived-at convictions, are also aware that there is so much more to be known, they will be willing to go on listening and being fair to other people, and so the creative circle will continue.

Figure 6.1 Coming to terms with new ideas and experiences

The importance of education in commitment

Protection against being indoctrinated lies in people developing their capacity for choice in such matters. Either one has chosen assumptions and values which have been thought about or one succumbs, through inertia and naivety, to the pressures of conditioning and indoctrination. As Wittgenstein noted:

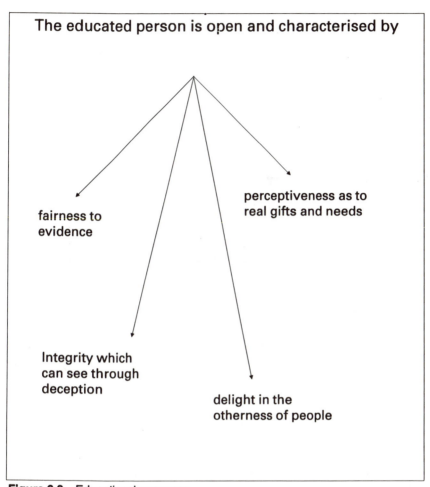

The educated person is open and characterised by

fairness to
evidence

perceptiveness as to
real gifts and needs

Integrity which
can see through
deception

delight in the
otherness of people

Figure 6.2   Educational openness

'The game of doubting itself presupposes certainty.' (Note 6, p. 84). Permanent indecisiveness and scepticism concerning every view is ruled out. Non-commitment on this matter always rests upon commitment in another, whether acknowledged or not.

The impression however should never be given that arriving at opinions which are true and valid is easy. Indeed the teacher needs constantly to draw attention to the complexity of the task, that in a sense it is a lifetime's occupation searching for that about which one can be legitimately certain.

One of the most urgent educational needs today is to engage students, from the infant years upwards, and including those in higher education, in a creative search for the assumptions and values by which to live. In this search, sincerely-held convictions must not be trivialised. Study in depth is required and a slow year-by-year development of understanding and skill in the handling of ideas, parallelled, for example, in the development of language skills. The controversial element must be central, and the assumptions and values of those responsible for teaching must be made available to those taught for scrutiny and criticism. In this living way education in commitment can take place constructively.

The education of commitment is not therefore a kind of optional luxury to be slipped into the curriculum if there happens to be time. It can free institutions from the inhibition of so-called neutral attitudes and permit positive teaching without betraying professional integrity. It will also challenge schools to work out the shared set of principles which alone can make an institution into a flourishing community.

The problem is that many people today are afraid of strong commitments. They are seen as fertile soil for intolerance, fanaticism and bigotry. A *New York Times* editorial on a speech by Solzhenitsyn, for example, commented: 'He believes himself to be in possession of The Truth and so sees error wherever he looks.' Note 7, p. 84).

Whether true of Solzhenitsyn or not, an extract from a seventh century writer puts the question of conviction in an entirely different light:

> Someone who has actually tasted truth is not contentious for truth. Someone who is considered among men to be zealous for truth has not yet learnt what truth is really like: once he has truly learnt it, he will cease from zealousness on its behalf. (Note 8, p. 84)

Indeed we would consider that the more a person is sustained by a certainty in convictions, the more s/he is capable of seeing truth wherever s/he looks. True openness is paradoxically only possible on the basis of firm convictions. The opposite of firm commitment is not no commitment, but a confusion of weakly-held or conditioned commitments, mostly unarticulated and imprecise. Free choice is crucial, but life does not wait for ever. Decisions have to be made on one basis or another. Not to choose is in fact to choose in a weak and unintended form, just as failing to answer a letter is itself answering it.

As already discussed (pp. 27–28), the first ingredient – essential to all the others which a child needs in order to learn – is the security of being loved and taken seriously as a person. It remains the prime underlying factor in motivation for students and staff. If this security is not present people tend to be incapable of relating for long to anything or anybody outside themselves. This deprivation is most marked in the young child, as all infant teachers know well. With older people it shows itself in a variety of ways: a need to dominate conversation and a corresponding inability to listen; being unable to attend to anything long enough to gain real understanding; a need to play a role most of the time and hide behind various fixed ideas; boredom and failure to get on the wavelength of what is outside their own immediate experience; disruptive behaviour of all kinds; obvious selfishness and possessiveness, ruthless ambition and so forth. This kind of behaviour indicates the absence of proper self-affirmation. Self-affirmation can be fostered – in those cowed by the impact of their backgrounds, upbringing and experiences from taking hold of themselves – by assertiveness-training, which has come to be much in vogue. Everyone does in fact have a duty to themselves.

Such affirmation is not just a matter of being open to people as people. It relates also to what people affirm, what makes them tick, their assumptions, their insights. It is therefore intimately concerned with questions of evaluation of values and the assumptions underpinning them.

What is insight?

Insight is a valuable word; it is used in a variety of circumstances, non-academic as well as academic, to point to knowledge felt to be self-authenticating, sure and related to experience. Insight denotes something very precious to a person. Insight is in what makes a person tick. People cannot deny their insights with integrity, and they react defensively if other people try to cause them to doubt those insights.

'To have an insight' is one of the most significant ways in which the verb 'to know' can be used, whether it means 'to know how', 'to know that' or 'to know a person'. It means to experience in a totally self-evident way an understanding of reality; that is, perceiving what actually is, or what reality is. In its simple form this is a very common experience. Insight is behind such expressions as 'Oh, of course!', 'The light dawns', 'Now I see' and so on. One of the most famous examples of the receiving of insight was when Archimedes suddenly discovered, while in his bath, his law about the displacement of water. He is reported to have run naked down the street shouting 'Eureka!'.

Usually, however, the process of acquiring insights is unobtrusive, slow and unnoticed by subject or observer, as when children accumulate the insights which enable them to read. This is why people sometimes say 'I feel as though I've known it all along.'

Some people show a greater capacity for the attainment of insight than others. As Lonergan in his important book on insight notes, such people are:

> marked by a greater readiness in catching on, in getting the point, in seeing the issue, in grasping implications, in acquiring know-how . . . . For insight is ever the same, and even its most modest achievements are rendered conspicuous by the contrasting, if reassuring, occurrences of examples of obtuseness and stupidity. (Note 9, p. 84)

Although insight is thus related to intelligence, it is important to note that insight is in no way the prerogative of so-called intellectually able people. Anyone, including any child who lives a fully human life, is capable of insights, however small. Insights evoke commitment, because the understanding gained is not just cerebral but involves feeling and will. Insights give stability and conviction to the person concerned and attach to themselves that sense of trustworthy certainty which human beings need if they are to become mature persons. People have a right to trust their insights, that is what they have come to understand through direct experience and/or genuine reflectiveness.

Discerning insight is not a straightforward, rule-of-thumb matter. People may, for example, imagine that they have seen a ghost, which turns out, on further inspection, to be a horse seen in certain atmospheric conditions (Note 10, p. 84). This is initial misinterpretation of a single experience. What is interesting, however, is that the conviction that it was a misinterpretation is itself an insight which can be trusted, and must be trusted if the people concerned are to continue to be rational beings.

This example draws attention to the way in which certainty regarding insights is cumulative and must take account of all possible theories – including the possibility of misinterpretation, that is, of calling by the name of insight what is in fact an illusion. Leontes in *A Winter's Tale* believed he had insight concerning his wife's behaviour and yet his whole vision had become warped by a demonic force of jealousy. The Delphic oracle was able to convey to him insight regarding his real condition, and this insight saved him, enabling him to sustain sixteen years of penitence for his wrongdoing.

Thus, although discerning insights is no rule-of-thumb matter, it remains true that only through insight can misinterpretation or oversight be appreciated. The safeguard par excellence against misconstruing insights is that four-fold quality of openness discussed above, together with a deep appreciation of the danger of ignoring or denying the insights of others. A genuine desire for a comprehensive view that takes in all aspects protects an individual from any severe form of deception.

Verbalisation of insights and its problems

Just as people should be on their guard against such misinterpretation of their experience whilst trusting their capacity for ongoing accumulation of insight, so they should be aware of the pitfalls in verbalising insights.

There is an important distinction between insight itself, derived from experience, and insight which is consciously presented to oneself and to others. Without entering into the enormous philosophical problems surrounding any attempt to define 'knowing' (Note 11, p.84), we believe it is necessary to appreciate the difference between what may be called 'inner knowing', which is often only semi-self-conscious, and 'verbalised knowing' – knowing which is clothed with words which seeks to express for oneself as well as for others what is known inwardly. This second kind of knowing has to wrestle with a host of hazards connected with language, intelligence, motivation, and so forth. They include the following:

1. Emotional involvement can tend to bestow on an experience a quality of completeness and absoluteness which does not properly belong to it. Each insight is by itself partial: it is wholly true but not the whole truth; it is valid

but not comprehensive. Yet it is easy to fall into the trap of seeing such an insight as the only thing that matters. This is because it is not possible to concentrate on, or be excited about, more than one thing at a time. We cannot listen fully to Mozart and Stravinsky at the same moment, or read a novel and a science textbook at precisely the same time. This point can be underlined several times if intense emotion is involved. Thus people in love, for example, often feel that everyone else is incredibly boring by comparison with the beloved.

2. Dependence upon vocabulary and thought-forms available to people exercises a highly constraining influence on the way they try to express an insight. People can use only those concepts which they have come across. Translation work constantly draws attention to this problem. Some people consider that fluency in other languages means that people think differently in each of them. Seemingly conflicting truth-claims can easily arise, when the real problem is lack of words available to use.

3. Words enshrine the accumulated experience of centuries but can easily become jargon and clichés. Such second-hand thinking presents a major obstacle to discerning insights. It is unfortunately all too frequent both in conversation and in academic work.

4. A related problem is the snare of misreading how words are being used. Care in recognising figurative use of language needs to be especially noted. There are many uses of metaphors which can be taken literally by those 'not in the know'. If someone speaks of a wet weekend, most people unacquainted with fairly recent colloquialisms in English would assume the speaker means it was raining, when in fact it may have indicated a miserable time.

5. The overtones acquired by words constitute a barrier to communication. For example, the word 'discipline', or even more obviously 'school', may be innocuous to one person, but act like a red rag to a bull for another. Words like 'democracy' are similarly 'loaded' with a number of overtones.

6. Overtones relate closely to the context in which words are spoken or heard. Context gives meaning to a statement: the insight indeed takes for granted much in the context, and often opposes just one aspect in that context which was found wanting. 'You've got to stand up for yourself!' is justified in a situation in which someone is being taken over or treated like a doormat, but if raised to the status of an independent principle, unbalanced by any awareness of the validity of other people's rights, it can dangerously encourage self-centredness.

7. A knowledge of context is particularly essential with regard to the use of overstatement in order to make a point more effectively. Doubtless this is often needed to enliven conversation, or give vent to strong feelings. To ban all emotive use of language would be as impossible as it would be counter-productive. It must be recognised as such, however, otherwise it

becomes itself a barrier in the path of those actually trying to discover the nature of other people's insights.

8. Insights are often inexpressible in words. As T.S. Eliot put it:

Words after speech, reach

Into the silence.

Words strain,

Crack and sometimes break, under the burden,

Under the tension, slip, slide, perish,

Decay with imprecision, will not stay in place,

Will not stay still. (Note 12, p. 84)

There is bound to be a considerable gulf between the original intuition and the reflection and eventual expression of it in words or action. To describe a bus journey may be easy, but an appreciation of a poem is not. Although we should have certainty in our experience, we should not be so sure of the verbalised form in which we talk about that experience. It is said of Beethoven that he would 'hear' a whole symphony in some ecstatic moment and would then have to undertake months of agonising hard work trying to get it right on paper.

This distinction between the trustworthiness of insights and the problems associated with expressing them in words is crucial; it is the distinction between 'inner knowing' and 'verbalised knowing'.

Critical affirmation

Learning such skill is part of the respect due to people and to oneself. It involves more than the openness discussed above and is better denoted by a term such as 'critical affirmation'.

The word 'affirmation' is a warmer word than openness. Its primary meaning is to make firm, strengthen, support, confirm. It has an essentially positive ring about it. In logic it is used as the opposite of 'negative'. It is a strong word which chimes in with concepts such as conviction, commitment, certainty. There is nothing vague about it, yet it is a welcoming word. Affirmation of people means acknowledging that they exist as living centres of reality; being willing to relate to them and appreciate all that is worthwhile about them, and confirming them in their status as persons.

Affirmation does not, however, involve being a rubber-stamp, saying yes to everything and losing one's own integrity. Just as openness involves at least four components, so affirmation must reflect a similarly comprehensive view and be directed not just to this person or that, but to all people in principle, to oneself, and to truth so far as it is discerned.

The apparent conflicts which such a comprehensive vision raises call for the exercise of discernment. The word 'critical' attached to affirmation underlines this. 'Critical' is used in the sense of 'involving or exercising careful judgement or observation' (*Shorter Oxford English Dictionary*) (Note 13, p. 84). By being attached to affirmation it loses the fault-finding, censorious, negative overtones which it so often has.

Affirmation and criticism, like openness and conviction, are not opposed. We can, for example, show respect for and affirm people as people precisely by taking them and their opinions seriously enough to disagree with them. To be critical of someone can in fact be one of the highest compliments we can pay, because it shows we are in active conversation, bringing our own personalities and insights into the meeting. Jane Austen, for example, in *Sense and Sensibility* writes that Elinor Dashwood agreed to all the foolish Robert Ferrars had to say because 'she did not think he deserved the compliment of rational opposition.' (Note 14, p. 84).

An attitude of critical affirmation gives us the capacity to deal creatively with controversy. It does this because it takes seriously the experience of other people, and the insights arising out of that experience, and seeks to affirm them whilst also affirming other experiences and insights including one's own.

Critical affirmation helps to build up a person by encouraging the search for trustworthy convictions which can give depth to personality. Indeed we are trifling with people unless we do have very great concern for our own and other people's integrity.

In summary, critical affirmation covers at least five intentions:

● the desire to find insight;

● the expectation that probably insights are there to be found;

● the determination to try to understand them;

● the rigorous use of critical faculties in so doing, not for the use of destruction, as though scepticism were the be-all and end-all, but for the purpose of creating a larger grasp of understanding and commitment both for oneself and for others;

● the desire to make other people's insights one's own.

The question may be raised as to how does this accommodate the various -isms discussed in Chapter 4? There is much of value in each of these -isms (see pp. 43, 45–47). The damage arises when they are believed in/accepted to the exclusion of other views and possibilities.

Note what has happened here. The -isms can be seen to be right in what they affirm, but wrong in what they deny when this is something positive arising out of other people's experiences. There is a distinction between insight on the one hand and oversight, blindness, hypocrisy, deception and ignorance on the other hand. The insights which it is desirable that another person should affirm must be searched for. A person is likely to present a precious insight embedded in phrases and patterns of behaviour which are not necessary to the insight. This is not just clutter, it may actually be destructive of, or negative towards, the insights held by other people or indeed other insights which the person concerned holds. This packing must be discarded and not affirmed.

We can in fact apply the analogy of light to a person's experience. Absence of experience can in this sense be likened to darkness. Moreover such non-experience is the weakest kind of evidence, for it can never answer the charge of possible blindness, only ignore it. By itself, therefore, the absence of evidence is unreliable. In Figure 6.3 the experience of someone who claims that pet

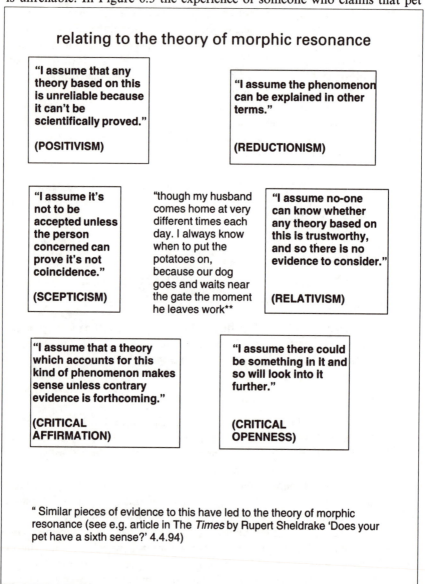

relating to the theory of morphic resonance

"I assume that any theory based on this is unreliable because it can't be scientifically proved."

(POSITIVISM)

"I assume the phenomenon can be explained in other terms."

(REDUCTIONISM)

"I assume it's not to be accepted unless the person concerned can prove it's not coincidence."

(SCEPTICISM)

"though my husband comes home at very different times each day. I always know when to put the potatoes on, because our dog goes and waits near the gate the moment he leaves work**

"I assume no-one can know whether any theory based on this is trustworthy, and so there is no evidence to consider."

(RELATIVISM)

"I assume that a theory which accounts for this kind of phenomenon makes sense unless contrary evidence is forthcoming."

(CRITICAL AFFIRMATION)

"I assume there could be something in it and so will look into it further."

(CRITICAL OPENNESS)

" Similar pieces of evidence to this have led to the theory of morphic resonance (see e.g. article in The *Times* by Rupert Sheldrake 'Does your pet have a sixth sense?' 4.4.94)

Figure 6.3 Differing reactions relating to the theory of morphic resonance

animals can have telepathic powers is referred to. It is important to note that their critics have not had the experiences. Therefore they have poor grounds for dismissing the interpretations of the experiences given by those who actually had them, unless other evidence is forthcoming which calls their trustworthiness into question.

Criticism is a negative activity by definition, so that although it has a justly esteemed place – indeed is essential in helping to guard against deception – it should never go off on a life of its own. For criticism always hides convictions which it affirms even as it hammers the convictions of others. This is why affirmation of other people is crucial. It calls for a positive tolerance which is very different from that motivated either by indifference to the truth, or by a search for convictions by those who think they have none. It gives the lie to the view that strong convictions and an open attitude towards others cannot belong together; in fact, the reverse may be true in that a person with strong convictions may be better able to appreciate those of others and accord them the careful respect they deserve. Moreover the attitude of affirmation can lead to a great strengthening of mutually realised convictions. The seeker after truth can never stand still; everyone is limited in experience and understanding.

> Listen to other people, and whenever you discern something which sounds true, which is a revelation of harmony and beauty, emphasise it and help it to flower. Strengthen it and encourage it to live. This requires from us a great deal (Note 15, p. 84).

This approach to controversial issues is possible but not easy. It requires great courage and a spirit of detachment when it involves, as it often does, affirming others who do not return the compliment. That is, affirming them in the face of being ignored, slighted or rejected. But the extraordinary thing is that one finds, in the end, that in affirming others one also affirms oneself. Many people find it difficult to like themselves – when they are honest they admit that they are highly critical of themselves without affirming themselves in equal measure. Paradoxically, genuine affirmation of others for *their* sake carries with it, as a corollary or unlooked-for offshoot, the capacity to affirm oneself. This is probably because if one learns to look for the good in others one can also see it in oneself.

It may be that readers consider this attitude of critical affirmation to be unrealistic. We commend it, however, as an approach which we have found to work regarding the meeting of widely divergent convictions and insights. We believe it does so because it takes seriously both concern for truth and concern for people, realising that people live by their insights but that over-sights, blindness, hypocrisy, deception and ignorance degrade the person who perpetrates them as well as his or her victims.

On the other hand, interest in others, the desire to know more and to widen one's horizons, and willingness to modify previous convictions so that they can become part of a larger and more comprehensive understanding, builds people up as authentic persons. In this way education can happen.

84

Notes

1. The quotation from Charles Peguy was quoted as the title of an unpublished paper by P.M.P. Cornall, 18 March, 1986, for a Schools Council Development Conference on the theme of Controversial Issues in School.
2. Bloom, A. (1987) *The Closing of the American Mind*, Penguin.
3. Dearden, R.F. (1981) Controversial value issues in the Curriculum, *Journal of Curriculum Studies* vol. 13, No 1.
4. Wake, Roy (May 1986) in the opening address to the School Curriculum Development Committee Seminar, entitled 'Contentious Issues in the Curriculum'.
5. Jeffreys, M.V.C. (1955) *Beyond Neutrality*, Pitman, p. 9f.
6. Wittgenstein, *On Certainty* 115, edited by G.E.M. Anscombe and G.H. Von Wright, Basil Blackwell, 1969.
7. *New York Times* 9 June, (1978).
8. Isaac of Nineveh quoted by Sebastian Brock in 'Isaac of Nineveh: some newly discovered works' *Sobornost* 8.1 (1986) p.30.
9. Lonergan, Bernard (1957) *Insight*, Longman, p.173.
10. I acknowledge discussion with Dora Ainsworth on this point, in which she referred to such an experience.
11. Ever since Plato raised the question, 'What is knowledge?' in the *Theaetetus*, it has continued to fascinate philosophers. See, for example, a very short article by Michael Welbourne, 'What is Knowledge?' in *Cogito*, January 1987, published by the Department of Philosophy, University of Bristol, pp. 12–14. The philosophical problems involved are well set out in *Knowledge* prepared by Tom Sorell (1981), Open University Press.
12. Eliot, T.S. *The Four Quartets: Burnt Norton V*, Faber and Faber.
13. *Shorter Oxford English Dictionary*.
14. Austen, Jane, *Sense and Sensibility*, Chapter 36.
15. Metropolitan Anthony of Sourozh speaking at a conference at Effingham, 1984, and reported in the journal *Sourozh*, Feb. 1986, p. 24.

Chapter 7

Organising Learning

How can the kind of approach outlined in this book so far be translated into classroom practice?

The overall purpose of values education is pupils' self-education, engaging in depth upon the basic assumptions concerning life and the values which necessarily emanate from the nature of the world of which we are a part. The understanding of values with which we are operating holds together both the subjective and objective aspects of the word: namely, what we or I value, and what we *should* value if we are to be in tune with reality as it is understood cosmically.

In actually delivering values education in the classroom, therefore, we have to ensure both genuine openness for reflection and rigorous academic enquiry. All children and students, whatever their abilities, backgrounds or experience have a right to this type of values education. This may seem a tall order. One anxiety should be disposed of right away however. To teach values education like this does *not* mean having to introduce a lot of fresh content. Mostly we can use what pupils are learning anyway.

It will of course take some *time*. It is a blunt pragmatic fact that priorities have to be decided upon, and that insistence on quantity undermines quality. To teach values education will encroach on the sheer quantity of content covered, but it is our contention that quality of reflection will more than make up for this. For example, to discuss in depth will result in pupils being much better motivated, and therefore better able to relate – and more quickly – to what they need to learn.

Pupils as expert learners

How do we reach such *quality* in learning? It is sadly true that much teaching, well-intentioned and carefully prepared, often gets in the way of pupils' learning. A character in *The Solid Mandala* by the novelist, Patrick White, explains this: 'I dunno', Arthur said, 'I forget what I was taught. I only remember what I've learned.' (Note 1, p. 99).

This neatly summarises a profound truth that teaching is about learning, and we only ever learn what we have chosen to relate to for ourselves. Only we can know when the time is ripe for such and such a piece of information, a skill, an understanding really to become part of us; meaningful and living. In the effort to make this happen for other people, teachers tend to take over – even in the most seemingly enlightened democratic and active learning approaches – because subtly, behind the scenes, the teacher has decided what it is appropriate for the learner to learn.

The chances of getting this right are remote – each child is unique; has unique gifts and problems; is subject to unique influences promoting certain aspects of learning and inhibiting others. Only the pupil can be the expert in his or her own learning, as babies demonstrate in their unaided learning of innumerable skills and knowledge and understanding.

The problem is also one of motivation. The most serious enemy of learning is boredom. One of the prime factors causing boredom is lack of ownership of what we are doing. We get switched off fairly quickly unless we ourselves see the point of what we are doing. If we are complying with other people's requests or dictates or constantly adapting, there comes a point quite soon when we just lose interest unless the material is tremendously entertaining, frightening or anger-making to us. Why it is always such a headache for teachers to get, and to keep, classes interested, is because there is something in the very efforts of teachers themselves which makes the attentiveness essential for learning harder than ever to attain. It is as though teachers are constantly pouring water into a bucket with a hole in it. However excellent in themselves the water or the bucket may be, the efforts are useless. Figure 7.1 may help to explain why, and to show the ideal which a teacher needs to have.

This chapter is based on the view that pupils learn easily, and that the efforts of teachers must be to get out of the way as much as possible. Their responsibility consists in providing opportunities for learning – a stimulating environment and access to materials that can interest and inform – together with a genuine concern for encouraging the self-responsibility for learning in each pupil. All other considerations of meeting requirements imposed by others or by oneself must be secondary to these two. In practice, other requirements present few problems if the first priority is allowing pupils the space and encouragement to learn what each decides.

The fundamental priority of giving space to pupils within an atmosphere conducive to learning relieves the teacher of a great burden which can rest on the shoulders of the more conscientious. No-one has unlimited energy, ability, time, and opportunity for study. None of us can do much more than simply brush the surface of knowledge.

The 'balanced' curriculum can never be one whose content is universally agreed or applicable. A child from a markedly scientific background needs a curriculum strong on poetry, whilst one who is versatile with words needs to learn scientific understanding to have a balanced curriculum. Everyone's needs are different.

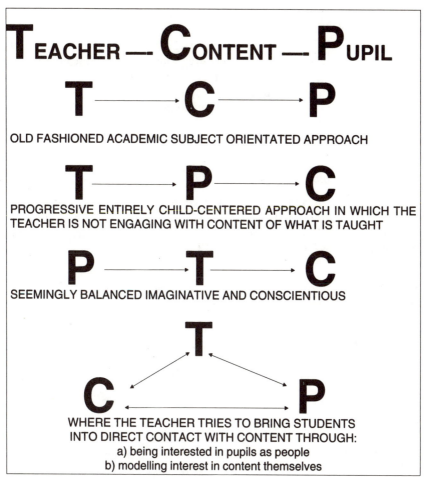

Figure 7.1

Requirements for effective learning

Affirming pupils as persons

Helping pupils to gain self-respect is essential if they are to have sufficient confidence and courage to move forward into the unknown. All learning involves taking risks.

Ensuring pupils have a sense of achievement and fulfilment

This could be attaining some self-chosen goal, or it could be the satisfaction of gaining further insight as one progresses, aware that gaining knowledge and understanding is like going on a journey.

Promoting self-assessment

The capacity for this is important not just because of the skills this gives which can be used throughout life but because everyone has to learn the ability to be self-critical without losing heart. The fact of limitations in ability and opportunity is bound, for everyone, to throw up situations experienced as failure, and these can easily torpedo learning. Pupils need to be helped to find satisfaction even in failure, through the way they cope with it, seeing it as challenge not as cause for depression.

Giving space to pupils

This is necessary, for unless they experience some real freedom of choice, it is hard to see how they can become responsible for their own learning. Space is also needed for reflectiveness and developing a sense of wonder. An element of spontaneity needs to be allowed for.

Providing a stimulating environment with sufficient structure and discipline to promote attentiveness

A sense of purpose and order is helpful in dealing with the ever-present problem of distractedness. To apply oneself deliberately and wholeheartedly to studying something, yet without tension, is far from easy. The capacity to do this lies close to the centre of effective learning, which can never just depend on things happening to be interesting.

Concern for appropriate pupil self-expression

We need to give plenty of opportunity for pupils to be able to express their understanding as it develops. Variety of method is called for, with encouragement to explore many different kinds of forms of expression according to a pupil's particular gifts and interests.

Abandoning concern for uniformity

This applies both to content and method. This does not mean abandonment of all control – the teacher's overall responsibility for pupils' learning remains, but teachers need to see themselves as enablers of pupils' learning, rather than constantly setting the agenda themselves. Furthermore, ownership of learning needs to be by individuals, not just by class consensus.

Listening to pupils and respecting their concerns and ideas

This is part of affirming pupils as people. It will also provide us with relevant starting-points for teaching programmes. A most important part of diagnostic assessment is relating to where pupils are now in order to help them achieve more. Patience and time are needed to ensure that we really hear what pupils are thinking, rather than settling for quick and possibly superficial reactions. It is not easy for many pupils to express their authentic thoughts. Often they have no experience of such conversation in their home backgrounds. Also they learn early about the wisdom of telling adults what they think they want to hear.

Modelling

Teaching by example, through actually being what one would like pupils to be, has always been the most effective way possible of communicating. For this inspires, and people learn most easily by copying what they are in the presence of.

Teachers must, so far as possible, see that all these nine planks for successful learning are in place and functioning well. This argues for an appropriate teaching style, one very different from that which looks for quick results and immediate impressions. It also argues in many people's minds for something quite unrealistic.

Possible objections

Play-school style?

An almost universal anxiety is that: 'Pupils, especially in primary school, cannot cope with this degree of freedom. They have to be *taught*. This fancy talk sounds fine on paper, but is quite unrealistic. It has been common knowledge for a long time that integrated work is not pursued with the rigour necessary to achieve any real standards in any of its component disciplines.' The HMI report in November 1991 (Note 2, p. 99) criticised this play-school style of education which is so prevalent in primary schools today. Giving children space means letting them do what they like, and that is not adequate. 'They will just waste their time and other people's, and public money, and not learn much either.'

It is important to note that we are emphatically *not* advocating such a *laissez faire* approach. The problem has arisen through an abdication of responsibility for promoting real learning to the fullest extent possible for each pupil. Structure and discipline *are* essential in order to build up the attentiveness without which learning cannot happen. And the insistence on modelling by the teacher is to underline the importance of inspiring pupils with an enthusiastic desire to learn. The style of teaching which we are advocating is certainly not a soft option.

The real point of the criticism of play-school-style integrated work has been the lack of seriousness conveyed through it. Wherever the core subjects have been presumed to matter, the integrated work is treated as an extra – to be enjoyable and interesting and to teach values of co-operation and so forth – but the level of skills and understanding to be achieved in the disciplines is often vague, and only valuable if one happens to be attuned to it.

But if this objection is satisfactorily answered, it leads straight into the opposite problem:

Impracticable?

Another common objection is as follows: 'For such teaching to lead to effective education, there needs to be at least three times the number of teachers working with very small groups and having endless time to give to each individual pupil. This is unrealistic. Staff shortages mean that even currently advocated ratios of staff to pupils are not met in many schools. So this is cloud cuckoo land.'

To this we would reply that, whilst increasing ratios of teachers to pupils would help, it is not essential and might even have disadvantages. Pupils need space from adults. Here are some considerations:

1. Affirming a pupil is often a question simply of a nice natural smile, a quick word of encouragement, a touch of humour, or an idea to think about, conveying the notion that we do care about the child for his or her own sake.

2. Children as well as young people are excellent at learning on their own – we only think they are not because they do not learn what *we* want them to, but what they authentically need and want to learn.

3. The stick-and-carrot approaches do not educate – they teach purely external responses irrelevant to the subject matter, and they can build up undesirable notions which effectively prevent real learning.

4. Children need space from adults, for learning happens most effectively when it is either spontaneous or self-planned. Insight comes only when it will – it cannot be commanded or controlled, or had on demand.

5. It is impossible to pass on one's own understanding on a plate to anybody. Teachers have always tended to think that if they say something long enough and in enough different ways it will 'get through'. Maybe parrot-like repetition is possible this way, but not understanding.

6. Content, in the form of precise facts which are known, is not important in the modern world – we each need to know many, many different things, and we need to know how to find out, and we need to know that we need to know them, etc. But no one else can give the precise facts which are needed for any one particular personal situation.

7. Only as adults are adults can they actually help the young to become responsible adults, otherwise a kind of in-house suffocation can result. There is a danger of adults becoming perhaps possessive and dogmatic, or

at least 'teacherish'. They too must have space to be themselves.

The style of teaching which is required therefore, is far from being idealistic. On the contrary, it is a most realistic way forward. There is a need for a *volte face* in our thinking. Our conception of education is still perhaps tied to something of the old monitor system, such as the grandmother of one of the authors experienced when, as an eighteen-year old, she had to teach sixty-seven pupils, and in one room!

Transforming the role of the teacher

Denis Lawton, Director of the Institute of Education in the University of London, considers the impact of the National Curriculum itself is likely 'to transform the role of the teacher. . . .' He goes on to say in what respect: 'The good teacher will no longer be just an efficient instructor, but will have to become an expert classroom manager and organiser of learning experiences.' (Note 3, p. 99).

What is required, however, is that teachers thoroughly understand the subtlety and importance of their task, and this involves being alert to a number of issues:

- the importance of the *received* curriculum;

- the question of indoctrination;

- the impossibility of a value-free stance;

- the need for appropriate methodology and organisation;

1. The importance of the received curriculum

Chapter 1 spoke of the *explicit*, the *implicit* and the *null* curricula, but the one which in the end counts is the *received* curriculum – what in fact pupils learn.

Immediately we are presented with a possibility – indeed likelihood amounting almost to certainty – that what we think we are giving pupils is not what they are actually picking up.

This can be very serious. A friend of ours became an anorexic through imbibing a message (mistakenly) from her father, who was a medical doctor, that it was bad to eat anything but fruit and vegetables. He did not teach this, but this, together with remarks about how awful it is to be fat, is what seared itself on her mind so effectively that, at the age of 40, though she knew it was mistaken, she still could not break free from it.

It is not usually just 1) *what* is said, but 2) *how*, and 3) *with what authority* on the part of teachers, and 4) *how often*, and 5) *what is missed out*, and 6) *in what context*, and 7) *with what personal attentiveness* on the part of recipients. Figure 7.2 expresses these as seven factors which can cause indoctrination: the

92

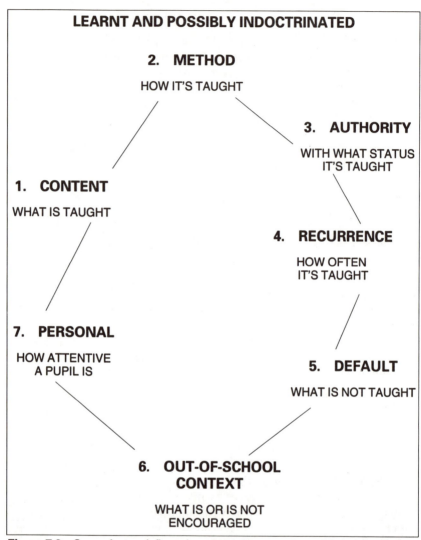

Figure 7.2 Seven factors influencing what is learnt and possibly indoctrinated

content, method, status, recurrence, default, context, and personal factors.

Pupil diversity carries challenging implications for teaching. Pupils from different home backgrounds will react in very different ways. Teaching, therefore, needs to have considerable flexibility so that the particular problems of each pupil can be properly considered.

Because this is so important a point, and has potentially very far-reaching implications for style of teaching, it might be helpful to consider some actual pupils that we can have in mind as possible recipients of teaching. Readers can readily supply their own lists.

DAVID: from a home in which both parents are professional and encourage him to think and be open to questions and experiences.

SHARON: from a home of well-meaning parents who have little idea about education at all – she is mostly left to her own devices.

GARY: from a single-parent home, economically deprived, where his main occupation is watching television.

JANE: from a home where a fundamentalist form of religion is pushed down her throat.

AHMED: from a home where the parents are genuinely devout.

EMMA: from a home where religion plays a very minor role (although she is pushed off to Sunday School), but the real priorities are consumer goods.

CHRISTOPHER: from a home where the Green Movement is very much in evidence.

HANNAH: from a home where parents are well-intentioned but over-anxious. She spends a large amount of time on outdoor pursuits such as horse-riding.

Values education is about getting all these pupils to think seriously about values. This is what they are entitled to: encouragement and sharing of skills to enable them to do this. For not to think about both what they and others value, and what is appropriate, offers a very poor reason for basing one's life on the values one has now. People are indeed deprived unless such possibilities are open to them.

2. The question of indoctrination

This question is discussed in Chapter 3 (see pp. 31–34). Whether real or imagined, indoctrination tends to be experienced as claustrophobia. This is a powerful ingredient of the negative attitudes which so many pupils have to schooling. These are compounded by many ingredients such as lack of self-esteem, fear of failure, lack of proper teaching of basic skills etc. A dull feeling that one is being got at, that somehow one is trapped within the thought and feeling patterns of others, is deep down a significant factor.

Teachers who are really educators take this most seriously and help pupils to a sense of freedom and self-responsibility. They acknowledge that all education is manipulation, except to the extent that it draws attention to that fact, and encourages pupils to think for themselves.

3. The impossibility of a value-free stance

It might help to look at this with regard to the suspicion which many have of a teacher who happens to have religious commitment. Many have expressed the view that this is a great obstacle to openness in teaching. Only when people are able to stand back can the bias, which is inevitably involved in commitment, not exert a baleful influence on what the teacher presents.

The impossibility of the teacher maintaining a posture of perfect neutrality was well expressed even 150 years ago by a Mr Wyse – wise for his time and ours. The prohibition of all interpretation would be

> . . . an absolute misnomer: instead of none it means any . . . it leaves it in the power of the teacher, or what is still worse, of the pupil, to take up the very first interpretation he meets. The very absence of interpretation may be proselytism. (Note 4, p. 99)

The teacher cannot, and should not, renounce overall responsibility for the learning. The authority of the teacher remains, and with it the unavoidability of conveying assumptions and values. But the way in which the teaching takes place is crucial, for it should always try to open up issues for pupils to reflect on, instead of closing the doors on such reflection.

The teaching style advocated in this chapter can effectively avoid the problems associated with commitment – both the teacher's and the pupils'. It can do this, not because it tries to banish commitment, but because the particular commitment of the teacher includes, at a basic level, commitment to those values and assumptions which are deeply educational and which contain their own safeguards against abuse. To use computer language, they are 'fault-resistant'. On this firm basis, the precise individual commitments a person happens to have can be educationally deployed without distancing the real issues.

Education cannot avoid advocacy as well as elucidation, but if the values it encourages are educationally valid – as those outlined in Chapter 1 – there need be no fear of *inappropriate* influencing by the teacher.

Many teachers have tried to get round the dilemma which still remains, of possible indoctrination into views which are challengeable, by constantly assuring the class that this is only their personal belief or opinion: 'It's just my view'. Unfortunately, in the present climate of opinion in Western society as a whole, this can easily be a form of conditioning in itself into relativism, as discussed in Chapter 4 pp. 46–48. It can be picked up by pupils as saying that there are no criteria available whereby the truth or falsity of a person's assumptions and values can be considered.

This is even more likely to be the effect if the teacher tries to act as a neutral leader. This appears to be highly educational – facilitating discussion by others without the teacher getting in the way by voicing his/her own opinions. Yet this oyster-like behaviour on the part of the teacher is almost bound to be regarded with suspicion by pupils. It in fact reinforces the divide between teacher and pupils which it is designed to try to break down, and can encourage a patronising, observing-from-the-side-lines attitude in the teacher. And pupils pick this sort of thing up quickly. Discussion becomes no more than a game for pupils – a way of passing the next half-hour – rather than a serious search for truth.

In all subjects the modelling of the teacher is a crucial factor. This extract from a conversation between a child and teacher about music teaching illustrates the point:

Q: What should we be telling other teachers about teaching music?

A: Not only just teaching music, it's like, not only teach, but teach them so that they *want* to be taught. 'Cause that's what you do.

Q: How do you mean, teach them like they want to be taught?

A: You were like, not just a teacher, you were like putting yourself into it, like, other teachers, they'd say, 'O.K., time for music class.' But you would say, 'Now, what do y'all want to do?' Things like, 'O.K., you know what I think?' Like showing your feelings and everything.

Q: Do you think that's important for other subjects besides music, or just music?

A: Yeah. A lot of subjects. *Every subject.* (Note 5, p. 99)

4. The need for appropriate methodology and organisation

A lecture given by Tim Brighouse at Lincoln in September 1989 began by drawing attention to some research done in Maine, USA (see Figure 7.3). The implications of this for teaching are worth pondering long and hard over. Is it impossible, for example, to have everyone teaching? And, failing that, active learning methods would seem to be far more effective than the ones which can easily make pupils passive.

This means that there should be maximum flexibility, and no attempt to expect everyone to do the same thing. Some pupils respond well to role-play and drama, or to collecting materials for display, doing photography or carrying out a survey. Fieldwork can often get pupils involved where in-school work seems to fail.

Work with computers offers many exciting possibilities and much more should be made of this, for it enables inter-active learning. But even without computers there is a great deal of other inter-active work that can be done using pencil and paper. Pupils can be encouraged to work out their own diagrams and mind-maps relating ideas to each other in visual forms, and by learning to work with *metaphors* and analogies. Various puzzles and games can also be very effective, especially ones which pupils work out for themselves or each other.

Probably the most effective general method is the project approach. This can take many forms, perhaps with a lead lesson and with a class working in groups or individually and pooling what they have done and found out at the end. The themes studied could be very different, even those running concurrently. The main thing is good motivation because self-chosen. This kind of

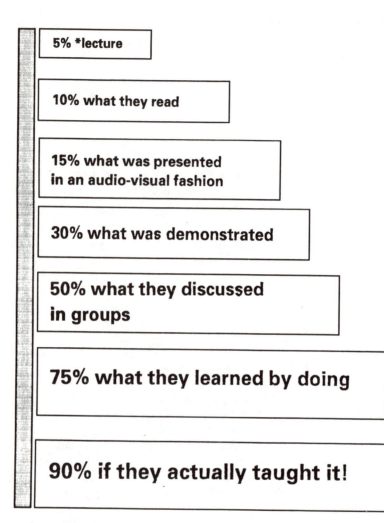

5% *lecture

10% what they read

15% what was presented in an audio-visual fashion

30% what was demonstrated

50% what they discussed in groups

75% what they learned by doing

90% if they actually taught it!

*5% learned what they had actually been told in the lecture.

Figure 7.3 How to learn. *Research done in Maine, U.S.A.*

approach gives the maximum amount of time to the teacher for contact with pupils and being able to engage in conversation with them, individually or in groups.

Of course for this to work there has to be a reasonable standard of discipline. Pandemonium simply creates distraction. So there needs to be a basic atmosphere of working and interest in the classroom. As will be developed in Chapter 11, involvement in interesting work is its own discipline.

Coming new to a class, maybe in a difficult area, and especially in the secondary school, can present quite a problem. There follow a few points which we would like to share on this.

- Whether the work is to take place in specific time allocated to Values Education (timetabled for example as General Studies, PSE) or whether it happens through the teaching of other subjects, it is helpful to begin by exploring basic questions such as, What is education? Why do we have schools? Do you enjoy school? Why? Why not? Is it important? Why? Why not? What is its purpose? What effect has coming to school had on you? Write down the questions you would most like to explore in school. What project would you like to do if you had the chance? How would you go about finding out about it? What values do you have? Where have your ideas about values come from?

- Such questions provide a natural starting-point for the pupils as well as for the teacher, whatever the class or composition or size. Depending on the teacher's personality and skills – what s/he feels happy with – it is better to do this with the class as a whole, perhaps writing up the results on the blackboard, or after an initial short discussion ask them to write this down without signing – so that it is anonymous. Carbon paper could be given to each pupil so that they can keep a copy themselves in their file and refer to it at the end of the year. In this way, they can see how far their ideas have moved; their concerns have been dealt with; their questions solved or rephrased.

- It would be important to spend a considerable time going through the replies with care to discover:

  common ground for most of the class – either content, questions or attitudes;

  specific interests and concerns;

  a likely range of ability, understanding and interests.

- Devise teaching around this analysis. Begin with something where there is common ground, and then move on to deal with the last point, via the second. Organise project work to be shared with the others and done either by individuals or by groups. Once some sense of cohesion as a class is established, there need be no unformity about content studied or ways in which individual or group projects are pursued.

- It is important always to read carefully what pupils write. For larger classes this is the equivalent of listening to them. It is equally vital, however, to ensure that they always write what they really think – authentic engagement on their part, neither towing a party line, nor using second-hand jargon, nor copying so-called facts from books. Conveying this to pupils is often not easy – so accustomed are they to giving what they think is wanted, or simply being lazy.

- The emphasis all the time must be on authenticity. We do not want cardboard pupils. But this means we must not be cardboard teachers! Modelling is supremely important.

- Teachers must always see they have sufficient space to be real persons themselves and not become over-pressurised. Integrity is one of the most valuable teaching aids, combined with a basic interest in the subject, and

Low Profile	High Profile
Cool approach	Warm approach
Critical	Affirming
Personally distanced	Involved and committed
Stressing objectivity	Stressing subjectivity
Intellectual	Emotional
Non-dogmatic	Definite
Asking questions	Giving answers
Learning with others	Teaching others
Acknowledging limitations	Confident
Non-interference	Taking initiative
Listening	Talking
Non-authoritarian	Exercising the authority of a teacher
Awareness of complexity	Clarity and simplicity
Reticence	Self assurance
Patience	Persistence
Not concerned with response	Expecting much
Take-it-or-leave-it attitude	Strong desire to help
Turning a blind eye	Disciplining
Concern for sklills	Concern for content
Voicing doubt and controversy	Voicing certainties and convictions
Stressing relevance to students	Stressing heritage of the past
Teacher subservient to routine	Teacher-controlled novelty
Acceptance of external norms	Inventive, creative approach to assessment
Stressing student experience	Stressing presentation by the teacher

This list is offered as a talking-point. The pairs are paradoxes not contradictions. The qualities listed under both profiles are needed in the same person for really effective teaching.

Figure 7.4 Paradox and the requirements of teaching

willingness to be real and vulnerable in the classroom. The teacher needs to get a measure of enjoyment out of the work and have a quality of self-respect which is the appropriate partner for the ability to assess oneself and resolve to move forward and improve.

Conclusion: 'Curiosity going on an adventure'

The teacher in the classroom is involved all the time in a balancing act. Teachers need to appreciate the subtlety of their role. A list of paradoxes is given in Figure 7.4 which expresses the apparent contradictions. There are no easy answers. The tensions we experience in teaching are many of them necessary and what life is about. But it is important that the tension is not destructive of people in a negative way.

For all of us, teachers and pupils alike, there is the possibility of progressive enlightenment if we are open to it. Whitehead (Note 6, below) spoke of education as 'curiosity going on an adventure', and classrooms need to be places where we can do just that.

Notes

1. White, Patrick, (1966) *The Solid Mandala*, Penguin, p. 57.
2. See e.g. article in *The Times*, 'Inspectors back return to traditional teaching', by David Tytler, 16 Nov. 1991, commenting on the publication of the HMI Report on the first year following the introduction of the National Curriculum.
3. Lawton, Denis, (1989) *Education, Culture and the National Curriculum,* Hodder & Stoughton, p. 86.
4. *Gladstone Tract*, p. 41, (1839), St. Deiniol's Library, Hawarden.
5. Upitis, R., (1990) *This Too is Music*, Heinemann, p.123.
6. A major theme in Whitehead, A.N. (1942), *Adventure of Ideas*, Penguin. See also Whitehead (1970) *The aims of Education and other Essays*, Macmillan Free Press.

Chapter 8

The Intellectual Capacity of Pupils

Stage theories and their critics

For at least three decades it has been fashionable to apply the psychology of Jean Piaget to the intellectual development of primary school children. As is well known in educational circles, Piaget defined a series of 'stages' according to which, he argued, the young must proceed before their development is such (on average at the age of eleven years) that abstract reasoning is possible. These 'stages' correspond roughly to the following:

- **Sensori-motor Period** (age from birth–eighteen months): development of reflexes.

- **Concrete Operational Period** (eighteen months–eleven years): this stage is divided into two phases the 'pre-operational period' which lasts until around the age of seven, when 'concrete operations' are being prepared for. During this time, children are said to be unable to conserve, and gradually begin to develop the facility to decentre, or see things from the point of view of others. During the 'operational' phase children are deemed to be increasingly developing the ability to internalise structures, based on 'concrete' objects and experiences.

- **The Formal Operational Period** (from about eleven years onwards): from this time children are able to reason in abstract ways and think logically.

It will be noticed that Piaget's 'intellectual stages' of development are associated with biological growth and development. He did not, however, rigidly insist that age was *necessarily* important: the ages when the stages are entered are offered as approximations only, but he did insist that satisfactory progress through each 'stage' was necessary if the succeeding phase was to be reached.

However, the psychology of Piaget has been very seriously criticised. Robin Minney (Note 1, p. 109, pp. 250–261) has pointed out that Piaget was a zoologist who also had an interest in epistemology: his PhD thesis investigated molluscs, and it is extremely questionable as to how far one may reasonably apply zoological studies to the development of the intellect. As Minney points out:

> ... there is potentially a big difference between the growth and development of the body and the growth and development of the understanding. Just to mention the 'savage' points this out: anatomically there is little difference between professor and primitive herdsman ... but the growth of understanding ... must be seen in relation to the environment in which this development takes place. (p. 251)

The development of the human intellect is a process so complicated and diverse that to attempt to confine it to 'stages' is to simplify dangerously what happens in reality. Such psychological theories can so easily lead teachers to classify children according to biological age rather than to look upon each as an individual who requires, therefore, individual attention and encouragement. To ignore this factor is to attempt to reduce the human being to an impersonal 'object' who is unable to think rationally and reason until the magic time when the stage of formal operations is reached. As is so obvious in any primary school classroom, children assert their individuality from a very early age, and the composition of this comprises factors which are biological, genetic, environmental, and social. It is the interplay of these, and the total reaction and assimilation of new experiences, which forms the character and personality. This process continues to develop and effect change throughout life, according to the opportunities which are encountered, and how individuals react to them.

Criticisms of Piagetian psychology, particularly the testing techniques which are used by researchers who follow his theories, have been described in detail by Margaret Donaldson (Note 2, p. 109), who points to the importance of children's limited grasp of language in their ability to perform set tasks satisfactorily. In addition, it has been pointed out by Ashton (Note 3, p.109) 1993) that children's ideas can be analysed according to criteria other than the scientific: even very young children think creatively, and will transcend the empirical realm into the metaphysical in order to postulate theories for natural phenomena.

Why did the psychology of Piaget become so pervasive throughout the educational system in Britain during the mid-twentieth century? Doubtless an important reason is that the theories provide neat, manageable ways of both organising and understanding young children of primary school age, at least superficially. The effects, however, have been recently described as follows by McNamara (Note 4, p.109):

> (Piaget provides) ... a licence for calling virtually anything a child does education. (p. 27)

Young children are energetic both physically and intellectually, and it is this drive which education ought to be developing, but in ways which are stimulating for creative thought. Countless numbers of school children have suffered boredom during, for example, lessons on 'People Who Help Us': such activities were advocated by educationalists who based their ideas on Piaget's theories (for example, Ronald Goldman, see Note 5, p. 109), and therefore argued that the primary school child's thinking was limited to everyday experience: hence schemes which investigated such saintly people as the Lollipop Lady, the School Nurse, and the Window Cleaner!

However, if one considers, for example, the intense interest which most young children have in dinosaurs, or the phenomenon of slavery in human history, the ludicrous nature of such theories is obvious, for which school child in Britain has seen either a prehistoric monster or a slave coming down the street?

It is, nevertheless, well known that whilst theories are very easily destroyed, they can be created only through painstaking observation and research. If – as seems highly likely – children do *not* in fact proceed through any type of 'intellectual stage', how do they learn, and to what extent can teachers hope to develop their potential for rational thought and reasoning through education?

Creative, rational thought and the school child

There follows a list of experiences which are common to all children of primary school age. All of these experiences have significance for the structure of lessons. You might find it helpful to list against each item any element within it which you feel could be useful when planning lessons.

1. Feelings of anxiety when losing sight of a parent in a supermarket or street.
2. Feelings of anxiety when arriving home and expecting to find mother/father in, but instead finding both are out.
3. Waiting for the promised visit from a friend who fails to turn up.
4. Worrying about the spelling test.
5. Lying in bed in the dark, feeling afraid of shapes and shadows.
6. Feelings of pleasure when you find something you thought you had lost.
7. The excitement of hiding, and wondering if you will be found.
8. Trying to dodge the bully yourself, or helping a friend to dodge him/her.
9. Feeling upset when you argue with your best friend.

Kieran Egan (Note 6, p. 109) has discussed how pupils attempt to make sense of their lives through the interplay of opposites which, he believes, provide the simple structure according to which they build concepts and develop understanding. All of the experiences listed above can be thought of in terms of opposites: that is, the structure of the experience, in abstract, involves tension between two extremes. Hence, the following apply to the above:

1. Lost and found; safety and danger.
2. Lost and found; safety and danger.
3. Looking forward with pleasure and disappointment.

4. Fear and satisfaction; safety and danger.

5. Light and darkness; fear and relief.

6. Lost and found.

7. Lost and found.

8. Safety and danger.

9. Happy and sad.

Egan argues that this is the *main* structure around which children build their conception of the world, and that, therefore, if lesson material is based upon the interplay of opposites – and the greater the number of opposites which are to be found in the lesson content the more interesting it is likely to be – the greater is the chance that the lesson will be successful.

This theory is very important, for it offers a simple explanation of why it is that young children – and no doubt adults – are able to relate to stories which are remote both historically and geographically. The story of 'Joseph and his Family' (see Figure 11.2, p. 146) is an example of this. What seems to be happening is that young children engage in rational thought from a very early age and base their thinking upon abstract elements which they extract from everyday experiences. This enables them to relate to extremely obscure material, provided that the basic structure is familiar and not too complicated.

Clearly, their thinking is not confined to experience alone, but rather experience needs to be considered by teachers to be a starting post from which lessons should move forward rapidly. Regarding Egan's theory of opposites, it is particularly important that children are helped to realise as they progress through Key Stage Two (in the National Curriculum) that life is, in fact, very much more complicated than black/white, lost/found, etc., and that certain situations and experiences – if not most – are a curious mixture of many opposites. Education should help them learn how to recognise these structures, evaluate them and grow to understand the reality of life more deeply.

Developing children's thinking in this way is introducing them to philosophical ways of thinking. Gareth Matthews, for example, (see Note 7, p. 109) considers philosophy to be an extension of play:

> Philosophy may indeed be motivated by puzzlement. But to show that and stop there is to suggest, quite mistakenly, that philosophy is inevitably something terribly serious. In fact, it is often play, conceptual play. (p. 11)

Matthews gives many examples of how the play of young children can be developed into philosophical thought. The following is one of them:

> URSULA (aged three years, four months): 'I have a pain in my tummy.'
> MOTHER, 'You lie down and go to sleep and the pain will go away.'
> URSULA: 'Where will it go?' (p. 17)

As Matthews argues, he cannot prove that Ursula had a twinkle in her eye as she questioned her mother for she could have been puzzled, or even worried, but the point she made is a philosophical question. Can abstractions such as pain, happiness and fear exist apart from the 'substances' of Aristotle, in perhaps the way that Plato described his Theory of Ideas or Forms?

What is certain is that the child could be thinking creatively, or alternatively that she could be asking an innocent scientific question. How the adult responds will have importance for how she grows either to understand, or misunderstand, the poetic use of language. I have given examples of this elsewhere (Note 3, p. 109) when analysing the theories of Piaget and ways in which his researchers interpreted children's ideas. Olivera Petrovich (Note 8, p. 109) has shown how even very young children will transcend the empirical realm into the metaphysical in order to provide a hypothesis, as mentioned above. What is suggested is that education should help to develop children's potential for reflective thought, both creatively and imaginatively.

The importance of this lies in definitions of what is meant, educationally, by *imaginative*. This word is frequently confused with fantasy, rather than speculation upon what could be, rather than what actually is: that is, the ability of extending powers of perception towards envisaging new possibilities coming into existence from old realities. It is not long since a child aged nine years said to me, 'I wish magical things could happen, instead of doing the same thing everyday.' Of course, magical things do happen daily, but the human propensity to accept such phenomena as 'normal' reduces the miraculous to levels of mundaneness, and the associated boredom and lack of vitality which, of course, will find outlets in other directions, whether in the excitement of burglary, drug-taking, or similar activities.

What is being advocated may be summarised as follows:

A brand of education which:

- recognises the individuality of each pupil and seeks to build up that individual's self esteem positively;

- seeks to base lesson content on structures of thinking which are familiar to children and yet which aim to extend them;

- recognises the potential of the individual for creative, philosophic thought from an early age and treats this seriously by developing lessons which extend imaginative insight creatively;

- searches for ways in which children may be encouraged to deepen their personal reflection on experiences generally.

Considering the ethos of the school.

It has been discussed how modern theorists have recognised the young child's potential for abstract thought through creative, philosophical discussion and activities, and how structuring lessons around the interplay of various sets of opposites is likely to engage the creative interest of pupils. Such teaching aims to encourage overall personality development. The subjects of the curriculum are a means by which this end is to be achieved. Young people are extremely lively, and it is the function of education, in its broadest sense, to engage this liveliness in activities which appeal to their natural curiosity. This process should be a continuous development through Key Stages One, Two, Three and beyond.

Please study the categories below, noting how they could contribute to lesson planning in the phase of education in which you are particularly interested.

FOUNDATIONS FOR STRUCTURING LESSONS

Excitement   unknown outcomes are stimulating imaginatively, but may work either positively or negatively for the life of the school.

- Examples of how excitement may form the basis for lesson content.

- Examples of how excitement may lead to unruly behaviour during breaks.

Mystery   problem solving structures offer challenges.

- Please note some lesson topics which could be structured around 'problem solving' activities.

- Could circumstances be created which would 'kill off' interest in problem solving?

Symbols   symbols often appear to be mysterious because of their hidden qualities and uncertain meanings.

- Please provide a few examples of symbols which could create a sense of mystery, and thereby prove stimulating, for classroom work.

- Symbols can also prove to be terribly boring: please suggest a few ideas of such symbols, and account for your opinions.

Predictions   predicting outcomes becomes exciting, especially when evidence is provided for analysis.

- Please suggest subject areas which could lend themselves to this method of structuring lessons, and perhaps suggest some topics.

- What criteria would be necessary to ensure that the children/students were not 'turned off' by being asked to make predictions?

The final section of this chapter provides examples of how these structures can be used to help pupils extend their ability to engage in reflective thought and use the results of such thinking as a means of developing their ability to use language symbolically.

Learning to use poetic language

In the foregoing sections, we have discussed how the thinking structures used by humans in their attempts to conceptualise and make sense of their experiences are complex and variable. This type of thought takes place throughout life, and educational activities, regardless of the subject being taught, should be encouraging children/students to develop this capacity further in ways which avoid the superficial patterns which are described in Chapter 4.

To do this, it is necessary to deepen reflective thought in numerous ways, including the acquisition of skills of literacy such as being able to recognise and use poetic language in both speech and written expression.

How far a developing ability to use language in non-literal ways contributes to the ability to think in increasing depth is something worthy of much discussion elsewhere, but what is certain is that the creative writing of many remains locked in set, wooden phrases which tend to make factual statements which do not reflect the thought which underlies the effort of expression. The following is an example, written by a nine year old:

> I heard something when we were on the rocks. I put my ear to a rock and heard a sound. My dad listened and he heard a sound. A man came from inside.

The ideas expressed are imaginative in the extreme: these include rocks possessing a life-force of their own, which is symbolised by the emergence of a human figure. The proof of this is emphasised by the witness of a respected adult, in this case, the father. However, there is much need to help the child develop her/his ability to use language in ways which are expressive of the deeper sense of mystery which stimulated the writing originally.

What should the teacher do in order to help the pupil's thinking and use of language extend and deepen? The answer lies in

a) linking understanding of the writing to the interest of the child in mystery and symbolism;

b) teaching both how to recognise metaphor in the writings of others and how to use it him/herself.

Much has been written on metaphor, and yet it remains one of the greatest mysteries of human creation. It is in debates about religion – its nature and forms of expression – which have probably led to some of the deepest misunderstandings in history. What, then, is metaphor, and how can teaching it break down the barriers between creative, internal thought and the ability of people to express their ideas in language?

Metaphor is a device in language whereby one thing is likened to another in order to stimulate comparison. The person attempting to understand a metaphor becomes actively involved in searching for appropriate meanings. For example, in the previous paragraph I used a metaphor: can you find it?

(The metaphor is, of course, 'break down the barriers).'

What does the metaphor mean? To readers, when they reach the succeeding words, it will become obvious that something is preventing children from giving adequate expression to their internal awareness and thoughts: this is the 'barrier', and its actual form is their inexperience, and lack of knowledge of how to use language symbolically. There are no barriers such as seas, mountains, or walls, although any of these could be used metaphorically when investigating the problem. The barrier is only too real, but is a barrier in a metaphorical sense.

This is not to say, however, that metaphor is untrue. The necessity of metaphorical usage lies in the fact that metaphor is a type of 'signpost' (and that is a metaphor of a metaphor!) which points to something which has reality but which is beyond adequate expression. It is for this latter reason that it is so necessary: if something transcends straight description, that fact does not point towards non-existence, but to *how things really are*, that is, to what has reality.

There are categories within reality which can only be understood by the giving of examples: such as things like happiness, friendship, anger. Regarding the latter, anger, a seven year old child once told me he had been in a temper that morning because of what his father had said to him. I asked him what being in a temper meant, and he said:

I felt that I had a fire burning, deep down inside of me.

The fact that he said the temper was a fire – that is by using metaphorical language to express reality – does not mean the temper was unreal. By comparing it with fire we can appreciate something of the force which it possessed, the danger, and the discomfort.

By discussing experiences in this way, pupils can quickly come to understand how metaphor works. Conversations of this type should not be confined to set language lessons, but developed at any time when the opportunity arises.

The following are examples of the work of ten year olds which was produced as a result of such conversations. The underlying teaching, carried out in diverse times and places, and in all subject areas, comprised the following:

- discussing abstract experiences and asking for ways in which they could be described;

- providing poetry and prose which used metaphor in exciting ways which related to the categories of mystery, excitement, etc.;

- using any incident at any time of the day in order to stimulate discussion and work on metaphor.

The following poem was written by a pupil who proved himself to be very quick at grasping the skills associated with metaphor. It should be noted that this boy had been in trouble constantly throughout school; he had much creative ability which had not been spotted, and he had, in consequence, suffered incredible levels of boredom and resentment!

Daffodils

Daffodils make me smile.
They make rainy days sunny.
But when they grow
Brown and weary
The whole earth
Sighs and is dreary.

When analysed, the poem shows itself to be quite profound. It should be added, perhaps, that the stimulus for this lesson had been the teacher asking a group of pupils to pick a bunch of dead daffodils for the classroom during the lunchbreak. This had caused much amusement and bewilderment. The flowers were discussed, and children were asked to close their eyes and to think what former lives the flowers had enjoyed. The Local Authority in this particular area had invested in planting daffodil bulbs extensively on grass verges and roundabouts, so the children had much experience to draw upon. What the lesson did was emphasise the significance of daffodils for human mood, in the few weeks following the bleakness of the winter.

This poem was written in response to a fly which some nine year olds discovered trapped against the classroom window. It was trying to escape. After discussion, this poem was written by Danay:

The Trapped Fly

The fly will try to get out
But there is no hope.
So hot, trapped –
As it dries and starts to die
It finally gives its last sigh
And its soul is free.

The value of these observations of the trapped fly was that the pupils' sensitivity was heightened. When someone suggested squashing the fly to 'put it out of its misery' there was a chorus of anxiety, to the effect that it had not done anything wrong, so why should it be killed?

What was of particular interest was the Platonic idea in the last line of Danay's poem. A few weeks earlier this girl had been interested in a print of Michelangelo's sculpture, 'The Death of a Slave', and at her request I gave her a few ideas about why the body was apparently trapped in the rock. Previously, she had thought the sculpture was unfinished. That the picture had been very powerful for her is reflected by her using its imagery in the fly poem. It might be comforting to know that at the end of the session a group of girls caught the fly in a paper towel and let it go free!

Conclusion

This chapter has introduced new theories concerning the capacities of even the youngest child for creative, reflective thinking, and the types of structures for lessons which are likely to be successful, based on the type of imagery which has been found to be stimulating for pupils.

The most important factor, however, is for the teacher to avoid theories which offer neat classifications of individuals on whatever grounds, whether chronological age, personality type, race, or social background.

All of the classroom work described in this chapter is suitable – indeed necessary – for all pupils, throughout Key Stages One, Two, Three, Four and beyond, because of the diverse forms in which it could be presented and because of the layers of thought which are possible according to individual temperament.

The psychology of even the youngest child is extremely complex, and to make assumptions about any individual is to court potential disaster. The most important view for the teacher to hold is that all pupils require help in their gradual acquisition of the skills needed for authentic thought: help which avoids the various pitfalls described in Chapter 4 and other places in this book. To offer this is to enable them to engage in the search for truth which was outlined in Chapter 3, and which is the goal for the definition of education argued for by the writers.

The excitement of classroom work is in discovering the most effective ways in which this can be reached. It is in the process of trying that pupils begin to be educators themselves.

Notes

1. Minney, R.P. (1985) Why are Pupils Bored in RE? – The Ghost behind Piaget, *British Journal of Educational Studies*, vol. XXXIII, No. 3, October, 1995.
2. Donaldson, M. (1978) *Children's Minds*, Fontana.
3. Ashton, E. (1993) Interpreting Children's Ideas: Creative Thought or Factual Belief? – A New Look at Piaget's Theory of Childhood Artificialism as Related to Religious Education .*British Journal of Educational Studies,* vol. XXXXI, No. 2, June, 1993.
4. McNamara, D. (1994) *Classroom Pedagogy and Primary Practice*, Routledge
5. Goldman, R. (1965) *Readiness for Religion*, Routledge & Kegan Paul.
6. Egan, K. (1990) *Primary Understanding*, Routledge.
7. Matthews, G. (1980) *Philosophy and the Young Child*, Harvard University Press.
8. Petrovich, O. (1988) An Examination of Piaget's Theory of Childhood Artificialism. (Unpublished University of Oxford DPh thesis.)

Chapter 9

Learning Strategies

Relationships

There can be little doubt that one of the greatest concerns of pupils relates to how well they get on with their teachers and with each other (Note 1, p. 123, pp. 178–193). If pupils are encouraged to discuss their first day at school, that is when they joined the reception class, it is common to be told that they worried about the teacher: reputations of individuals are eagerly passed on from one pupil to another and often become distorted in the process. For example, Peter admitted:

> I cried myself to sleep before going into Mrs Davis' class. My friends told me that she shouted at you when you got your sums wrong, even when she never showed you how to do them.

Sharon's fears echoed those of Peter:

> Everybody called Miss Lewis a witch: Ganny Lewis, they used to call her. That was because she always dressed in dark colours. They used to say her classroom was really a witch's den.

However, Lisa's anxieties focussed on her peers, and were reflected in many of the other pupils' ideas:

> I worried that when I started at school I wouldn't have any friends and that people might laugh at me. At playtime I went and stood in a corner, but this girl came up to me, and she said 'Want to play chasey with us?' and it was all right.

Such ideas need to be dealt with positively, whatever the age of the pupils concerned. Younger children, because of fear, can easily be distracted from their work, whilst older pupils are likely to 'play the system': that is, to test the teacher in order to see how far they can go in attempts to disrupt the work of the classroom. The age at which this latter occurs is, in fact, becoming increasingly younger: it is not long since one of the authors heard a five year old remark to a peer, 'Its all right; she cannot do anything to you', which fact seemed to give full licence to be as naughty as she pleased. This, in fact, supports our view that conceptions of corporal punishment have been the main-stay of our educational system for well over a century, and associated attitudes are quickly passed on from one generation to the next. Some radical rethinking is necessary, therefore, in order to move perceptions of what education is about on to a more realistic plane: that is, where the teacher is perceived as being the supporter, confidante, and otherwise 'friendly, wise ear' for the pupil. It is only under such conditions that true education will develop.

Here is an example, taken from recent experience. When visiting a class recently, an experienced teacher sat beside two nine year olds. One of the boys leaned over to her and said 'We're the 'ardest (toughest) lads in this school.' The teacher immediately responded, with a loud laugh, 'Well, watch it lads, because I'm the hardest teacher in Hartlepool.' The boys laughed spontaneously *with* the teacher, and the ice was broken through the mutual exchange of wisdom! When she visited the school on other occasions, both boys greeted her. Had she been a teacher in that class, there could be no doubt that they would have been friends.

Where should they sit?

Many discussions have ranged over many years about the seating arrangements of classrooms – should the pupils sit in rows or in groups – and even whether it is necessary, or even desirable, to have a chair for everybody. Some teachers have even dispensed with their desk in efforts to accommodate the latest ideas. However, how far such decisions are *educational* are highly questionable. Of much greater significance are the individuals who will be seated in whatever arrangement of tables and chairs the teacher agrees to.

The last three words of the preceding sentence are of central importance to this section, for even the tables and chairs in a classroom provide the opportunity for educational discussion and decision-making. Lacking in educational value are situations where the pupils are allowed to sit anywhere, because this lack of order can very easily degenerate into anarchy.

What is desirable is that the teacher should pass on to the pupil the responsibility for where s/he sits, and for how long the arrangement will be able to continue. This is because such opportunities – and they arise in many diverse forms – enable the teacher to share with the pupils many of the assumptions and values which underlie decision making. Thus dogmatism is avoided as are the undesirable results which so often develop. This is particularly important because of the negative effects which dogmatism has upon relationships between pupil and teacher.

DISCUSSION: How would you respond to the twelve year old who came up and asked if he could move his seat beside Billy? (Billy is a talkative child who is well known for distracting others.)

Whilst numerous responses are possible, perhaps not too many of them have the potential to be educational! Those which manage to qualify for this category are those which cause the pupil to make some decision on the basis of commitment. A possible conversation with the teacher could develop like this:

Conversation 1.

P. Please, can I move my desk beside Billy?
T. Why do you want to sit there?
P. Billy is my friend.
T. Do you think you might both talk too much and not get your work done?
P. I promise I'll do my work and not talk.
T. Well, I'm not sure, but you can give it a try for a few days and see if you can both manage it.
P. Thanks.

Please evaluate this conversation (similar ones take place daily among teachers who use such opportunities for educational purposes), by listing the assumptions which lie behind the values expressed (see Chapter 4). How far do they contrast with those found in the following conversation?

Conversation 2.

P. Please, can I move my desk beside Billy?
T. Of all the people in this room, Billy is the last person you should ever sit beside. Of course you can't. Go and sit down.

Conversation 1.

Assumptions:

1. that there could be a teaching opportunity here – perhaps both pupils could learn from their decision to sit together.

Values:

1. it is right, and desirable, that pupils should take responsibility for their own decisions;
2. that opportunities should be created from pupils' interests which have a positive focus;
3. that trust is something valuable and which needs encouraging; it is important for pupils to learn skills of self-evaluation.

What the pupils will learn:

- it is up to Billy and myself to make sure we get our work done or else we'll have to move seats.
- I am responsible for myself.

Conversation 2.

Assumptions:

1. that pupils should obey teachers;
2. that pupils are incapable of taking responsibility, even for themselves;
3. that pupils cannot be trusted.

Values:

1. that the teacher should be in control and ought to be obeyed by the pupil;
2. that the 'immature pupil's judgement' is inferior to that of the teacher.

What the pupils will learn:

- that teachers are bossy;

- that teachers do not trust pupils;

- that they may as well misbehave and play the system by enjoying the fun of fulfilling the negative role allocated them by the teacher.

It will be noticed that none of the above examples includes any direct teaching of subjects of the school curriculum, and yet they easily become examples of how curriculum studies can develop from simple, everyday incidents in the classroom, and because of these origins of interest, which arise from pupils' own interests and concerns, are likely to be extremely effective teaching and learning strategies.

Relating learning to pupils' ideas

Not everything which concerns or interests pupils will emerge during the typical day in the classroom, although sometimes younger children will volunteer information which can be used to initiate schemes of work. At times, written work can reveal the kinds of things on which pupils are reflecting and which can so easily be missed, and so fail to provide educational opportunities.

As examples of this, there follow extracts from pupils' writing which offer much opportunity for educational development. Please make notes on each, indicating the educational implications and type of lessons which could result in order to help the pupils understand *at greater depth* the implications of the topics.

SHARON'S STORY

I was on the beach with my nana and my mam. We were coming down the stairs and I had to help my nana because she could not get down very well. We saw a dinosaur and my nana just went up the stairs like a shot and it was the fastest I ever saw her go up stairs.

LEE'S STORY

> I wonder about my dreams because when you are falling asleep it is just pictures in your head. Why, when you are asleep, does time seem to fly?

Sharon's story raises a number of points which could be taken up in discussion:

- Why do older people sometimes have difficulty walking?

- Was the child likely to have felt irritated at having to help her grandmother, and could she have invented the dinosaur as a metaphorical way of saying her grandmother could have moved more quickly if she had wanted to?

- Was the dinosaur a metaphor of her wishful thinking: that her grandmother could suddenly become young again, and able to move easily as a result?

Obviously, much work could result from Sharon's story, particularly about the need to be patient with elderly people. There is a need for this teaching focus because it acts as a balance to media propaganda. Television programmes and the advertising industry in particular, frequently present the elderly as a vulnerable group.

An effective approach could be to trace the problems associated with old age or infirmity and how the human race has attempted to deal with them in past ages: for example, the workhouse system; looking after elderly relatives in the family home; the incidence of rest homes and hospitals in the area, and the importance of talking with older people about their experiences of life generally, as a means of learning about the past.

Such development helps pupils reassess their assumptions concerning elderly people – which, albeit subconsciously, they have begun to accept – and to redefine the values which they hold as a result. Similar teaching strategies can be used for dealing with many controversial topics, ranging from animal welfare to the analysis of truth claims in science.

Lee's Story

Most people are fascinated by the subject of dreams, and will talk freely about their experiences of them. Lee's writing raises the following points of interest:

- What is a dream?

- What is time?

- Do dreams have any particular significance?

Lesson material could include the following:

1   the story of 'Joseph and his Brothers' (see p. 146), analysing the idea that dreams can be used to foretell the future. Can the children offer any examples of this from their own experiences?

2   teaching about the various dimensions of time: past, present, future, and eternity. Which of the first three is the strangest? Some would say the past because it cannot be changed, others the future because it has yet to happen, and yet others the present because it is so short! The concept of eternity can usefully be taught in connection with astronomy, and the history of measuring time: What are we actually measuring? Is it real, or something made up by humans?

The value of such work includes the elements of creativity which are offered (see Chapter 8) through the dimensions of mystery which they all encapsulate. However, the over-riding importance of work of this kind is the reflective thinking in depth which is encouraged and the effects which such has on personality development. Pupils are helped forward in their thinking by being offered new ways of approaching the familiar, rather than being left in a mental position from which there does not appear to be any means of escape other than abandonment.

Focussing on lesson content

a) Schemes of work

It has been discussed in Chapter 8 how it is probable that young people think and learn within a structure of opposites, based within contexts which are exciting and mysterious. This is especially true in the early years of schooling, but throughout adolescence and into adulthood students will conceptualise and develop values as a result of material which engages their interest. In later stages of schooling it is essential to help pupils understand that life is extremely complex and that it is frequently very difficult indeed to evaluate whether someone or something is good or bad, true or false. For example, pupils can be posed with a problem from history which continues to present horrific problems for today. An example is the question of poverty, a scheme of work for which is given below.

Scheme of work: The Poverty Problem
(End Key Stage 2/Key Stage 3 Pupils)

Appropriate aims:

● to examine the diverse causes of poverty;

● to help students reassess their own assumtions;

● to involve students in discussion through the medium of problem solving;

● to explore how humans have attempted to understand and contain the problem over time;

● to help students begin to make reasoned judgements on the basis of evidence, and to form values as a result;

- to encourage attitudes such as understanding, sympathy, and the necessity of trying to alleviate suffering.

Teaching strategies:

- whole-class teaching;

- group discussion leading to decision making and the production of display material, together with individual work.

Historical aspects:

- presenting groups with primary source materials, e.g. population statistics, extracts from documents, etc. and asking them what they would have done if they had been in the government of the time. Reporting back their ideas to the others, and then the teacher explaining what actually did happen, with the next few lessons following this pattern.

Social problem of poverty today:

- class discussions about beggars and homeless people seen on streets;

- reasons for poverty, from pupils' perspectives.

Anticipated outcomes:

- greater understanding, on the part of students, of the underlying causes of poverty;

- some understanding of the role of government in attempting to deal with social problems;

- through discussion, and the sharing of ideas, the encouragement to think reflectively and in depth concerning important human issues.

It is not difficult to see how such a scheme of work could develop (particularly through studies of poverty in Britain today); the questions which it raises, and how authorities are attempting to cope with it. Of particular interest could be to discover how pupils themselves perceive the causes of poverty, both before and after the teaching scheme.

Work done in depth, engaging the interests of the pupils by attempting to understand problems through time, and how human beings have tried to solve them, goes some way towards encouraging genuine thought and understanding of the real issues involved. Because of the depth of study possible, assumptions based on the various '-isms' described earlier in this book, will be guarded against in preference to meaningful discussion based on evidence.

When asked to discuss what the causes of poverty might be, Key Stage 3 students came up with the following responses. Please analyse which of the '-isms' (Chapter 4) could have been influential in the forming of the opinions, and the confusion between different types of poor, that is, between beggars and others.

- They are bone lazy.

- They spend too much money on beer and tabs.

- Some people just hate work.

- People like that make their own friends and live apart from others.

- They have a right not to work if that's what suits them.

- We have no right to judge them: its up to them.

- They might as well beg and get money like that if they can. They might enjoy the fun of it.

What types of evidence could be produced to help the students refine their value judgements?

b) Language work through imagery

Almost any subject takes on the attributes of mystery and excitement if it comprises unknown outcomes, particularly if related to phenomena whose origins are uncertain. Lively, stimulating approaches to teaching and learning can be created by relating, wherever possible, lesson content to such patterns.

Natural objects are well known for the power they hold over the human imagination. Such phenomena as rocks, stones, trees, water, mountains and so forth are well known symbols in literature for many aspects of the human psyche. Theories of why this is so were formulated, among others, by Carl Jung, who called the images *archetypes*, or the images used by the collective unconscious to manifest itself. Whether or not Jung's theory of archetypes points towards the reality of the mental life of human beings, there can be little doubt that most people will respond readily to aspects of the natural world, and for this reason teaching schemes which use these images are likely to produce effective learning. For example, it has been found that rocks and stones are powerful symbols for the imagination of ten and eleven year olds (Note 2, p. 123), whilst human creations *based on* natural phenomena, for example The Green Man, produce similar effects (Note 3, p. 123).

In order to help pupils express their ideas, it is necessary to teach how imagery is used in language (Note 4, p. 123). An effective way of doing this is to provide examples from the world of literature. After studying the seventeenth century poem by Thomas Campion, *There is a Garden in Her Face*, the pupils (eleven year olds) and teacher discussed what the title could have meant: did 'she' have plants and so on growing out of her skin? If not, in what other ways could a face be like a garden. Various suggestions were put forward: they were unsure of what time of year it was, and that would make a difference: a garden in winter was quite different from a garden in spring. Why? – because a winter garden is full of dead things, but in spring, a garden is full of life. These discussions and ideas were helpful. The teacher asked the pupils for suggestions for a different poem, something like *There is a Garden in Her Face*, and after a few suggestions Steven came up with *His Face is a Thunderstorm*. Without further discussion, the class were given a few minutes to try to set out a few thoughts. The following lines provide examples of the outcome:

His Face is a Thunderstorm

His eyes are lightning, flashing away,
His voice a bulldog, held at bay.
His face is the thunderstorm, evil and bad –
His smile the sun – hidden among clouds –
Never seen.

His Face is a Thunderstorm

His face is a thunderstorm
Making thunder in the sky –
It shakes the ground,
Makes me cry.
His face is a red fire,
Throwing balls at the ground, and
As he fades away
I look all around.

The pupils had understood the idea of characteristics of one thing being able to illuminate understanding of another: in the case of lightning, its ability to scare being similar to the effects of bad temper. By making the comparison, their insights into the nature and effects of temper – negative and potentially destructive – had been stirred into full consciousness.

In a similar way, the poem *Days* by Philip Larkin was shown to ten year old Colin. He wrote the following; probably the most effective piece of writing which he had ever produced:

Days

Days give me the feeling
About living and dying –
Like in the night when
You cannot move or speak.
You are in a different zone
While in the day you move,
Speak and do things.

Probably the points from both poems which were used as examples of metaphor and which excited the imagination and creative thought of the pupils were: firstly, the natural imagery, that is of gardens and lightning, and secondly, regarding *Days*, the mysterious nature of time's passage.

It is through such lessons, which engage children and students with subjects in depth, that their understanding not only of language, but of the human situation in general, is helped to deepen and mature. It is through this process that their values, and the assumptions upon which they are based, are refined as their capacity for reflective thinking develops.

c) Using the urban environment

The urban environment abounds with subjects for topics which can be used as stimulants for learning, and which can be developed in varieties of ways. For example, the subject of *People* is difficult to exhaust. There follows a list of topics the titles of which themselves suggest exciting lesson content:

- Beggars and Vagabonds
- Out Shopping
- Trying to Sell Things
- Should I Buy It?
- Drivers

In addition, if familiar subjects are given a focus which has an inherent feeling of mystery, the eager response of pupils to investigate it further is assured.

Here are topics which are familiar to urban pupils, and which, if presented under the titles written below would, in all likelihood, produce an immediate 'switch off' to enthusiasm. Perhaps the reader would like to suggest new titles, based on the ideas for stimulating pupils' interest given above.

- Transport
- Buildings
- Shops
- My Street
- Houses

Suggestions for improving the images of the above schemes of work are:

- Moving To and Fro
- Bricks, Cement and Spaces Between Them
- Can I Sell? Should I Buy?
- A Road is Like a River . . .
- Who Lives There, I Wonder?

Whilst they certainly are not perfect, we suggest that the latter titles would help pupils think creatively in new ways about familiar scenes and objects. This should enable the old to take on new dimensions of meaning because of the new ways of interpretation offered. For example, by changing 'Transport' to

120

'Moving To and Fro', the image of buses, cars and lorries is offered a symbolic extension through inviting the children to make comparisons, as happened in the poetry lessons analysed briefly above. This is the idea behind changing 'My Street' to 'A Road is Like a River . . .': the mind is immediately led to wonder how a road can be thought of in terms of a river, and the comparisons begin.

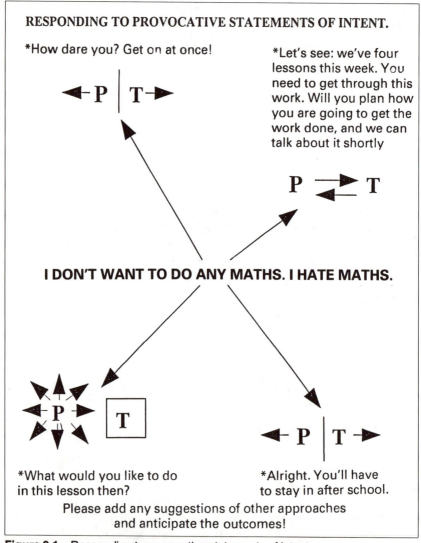

Figure 9.1   Responding to provocative statements of intent

Coping in the classroom

It cannot be stressed too strongly that the way in which the teacher responds to pupils can be crucial for the ensuing relationships which develop, and also for education to take place. There can be little doubt that in an age when authority – in its many forms – is constantly being challenged, education is most unlikely to take place at any serious level, or in a positive manner, unless pupils are given freedom to focus in depth upon their own interests and concerns. Education should help them develop positively through growing sensitivity and awareness of the rights of others to expect equal respect and freedom (see discussion in Chapter 2).

PUPIL: Please, I don't want to do any maths. I hate maths.

Responses to pupils' statements such as this, particularly older pupils, pose a challenge to the teacher. How would you respond? Figure 9.1 provides some responses and are what the writers would predict as being the results of each one offered. Do you wish to offer additional ideas? Which of the '-isms' are underlying each?

Planning activities

Can you imagine what it must be like to:

- be forced to work in a group all day;
- do nothing but listen to someone else talk;
- fill in work sheets each lesson on mundane topics;
- have to 'find out' all the time and never being taught?

Figure 9.2 provides ideas for varying the format of the activities of the school day. However, such should not be seen as replacements for the teacher, but simply supportive activities/resources. Can you add others? The typical school day should be varied, according to the best and most appropriate way of encouraging effective learning.

Conclusion

The role of the teacher is extremely complex. However, it is not the role itself which is so diverse, but rather the diverse ways in which the role can be carried out. Young people learn constantly, both in school and outside of it, but what they actually learn can be quite different from that which is taught (see Chapter 1). One of the skills of teaching is the ability to decide on which strategy is

122

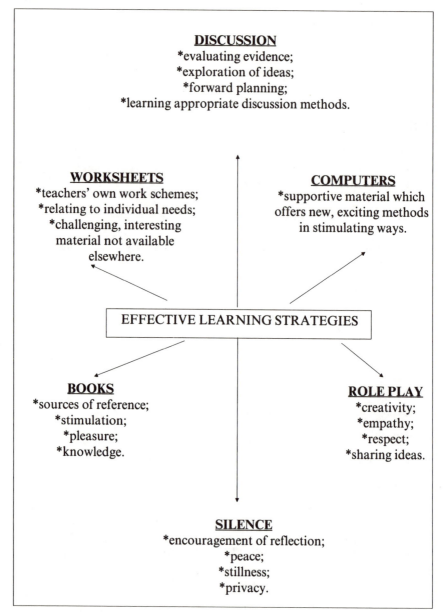

Figure 9.2

likely to be most effective for particular students or children – and for the
specific subject content which is to be taught – and the effects which this is
likely to have upon individual development. Nevertheless, subject content is
not the only medium through which human beings learn. As a last word, we

offer this true anecdote from personal experience, and ask the reader to draw his/her conclusions from it as to what the particular pupils concerned learnt from the teacher:

CASE STUDY

Mrs Scott was a primary school teacher of many years experience. One of the pupils at the school lived in a village some three kilometres distant, and cycled to school each day, accompanied by her border collie dog, Rover. Rover guarded the girl, Jean, on her daily journeys, and whilst she was at lessons, lay beside her cycle, growling at anyone who ventured near.

Mrs Scott was always terrified of the prospect of any of the pupils getting bitten at breaks, and winter or summer, whether on yard-duty or not, she spent each break sitting on the school wall, near Rover, with her cup of tea. This way, she could ensure that none of the children teased him and got either themselves or the dog into trouble. It was common for people who lived in the village to see her talking with pupils, some of whom sat with her on the wall during the breaks, with the dog lying watchfully nearby.

Notes

1. Cullingford, C. (1990) *The Nature of Learning*, Cassell.
2. Ashton, E. (1993b) Rock of Ages, in *Questions*, Summer, 1993.
3. Ashton, E. (1993a) The Green Man and Religious Education, in *R. E. Today*, Spring, 1993.
4. Claxton, G. (1990) *Teaching to Learn*, Cassell.

Chapter 10

Attitudes to Testing, Assessment and Examinations

Analysis of procedures

Ways by which educators can record, assess and examine pupils' educational achievements raise some difficult questions, not least of which is how far what is recorded, assessed and examined reflects accurately what pupils have actually learned – and the younger the child the more difficult the task often appears to be.

The reason for which schools exist is discussed throughout this book, and how the context within which the educational system of this country has been planned is the personal development of pupils in its various aspects. The significance of this 'educational context' is immense: if this is the purpose of education, should any recording, assessing and examining of pupils' progress be extended to an appraisal of the whole of a pupil's development, rather than relating solely to that which is more tangible, namely subject knowledge and the acquisition of skills? If so, precisely *what* details should be recorded?

What are necessary, of course, are examination syllabuses and tests which reflect the context of education of the Education Reform Act, 1988 *and* subject content. The two need to be welded together in ways which are realistic, helpful and manageable by being explicit as to the purpose behind the particular work scheme. However, for this to be possible, a carefully-structured context of Attainment Targets and Statements of Attainment in subject areas which have *built in to them* education in beliefs and values is essential.

Figure 10.1 provides ideas about how teachers, especially those in the secondary phase of education, can help young people begin to face and understand why examinations and assessment are built in to the educational system.

Any methods of assessing, examining and recording pupils' work are easily misunderstood, particularly by those who are not involved in education themselves. It is for this reason that it is wise for teachers to ensure that parents, especially, understand the remarks written on pupils' work, and the

FOSTERING POSITIVE APPROACHES TO TESTS AND EXAMINATIONS

Preparing for tests/examinations:

*discuss with children/students the work which has to be done;
*the purposes behind tests/examinations;
getting a job; finding out what you know;
how they help in planning your future work;
*preparation is disciplinary itself;
*the work can provide new ideas/stimulation.

At the test/examination:

*it can be good to know that you have prepared well for it and can respond in an orderly manner;
*it can be stimulating to assess your own performance;
*it is good when it is over and you feel free to do other things!

OVERALL:

*it is good to have aims;
you 'know where you are going';
*it is exciting to make achievements;
*often moving forward from the achievement can be stimulating in itself.

Figure 10.1 Fostering positive approaches to tests and examinations

educational purpose of such documents as the school report. This point is illustrated by the following conversation, overheard recently by one of the writers.

Two mothers were talking at the bus stop. The child of Mother A was in the Reception Class, and the mother told the following story to her friend:

> Mother A. I was speaking to Mrs Y the other day, and she told me that her Denise had five 'very goods' written on her exercise book. I went straight home and counted our Susan's, and she had twelve 'very goods' and a silver star.

This brief monologue raises a number of points. Please list them, according to what it teaches the teaching profession about parents' perceptions of the work of their offspring in school, and what should be guarded against when both assessing progress and marking work.

We would raise the following points:

1. Parents, understandably, will use any available means to compare progress, without necessarily understanding the data they use: perhaps Susan was merely being given extra encouragement by her teacher because she was slow?

2. Parents can easily be misled about the nature of marking and testing procedures; dialogue needs to take place between them and teachers concerning the methods used to give encouragement, and how such relate to individual, rather than comparative performance. Plans for teaching for the forthcoming term could usefully be submitted to parents after each break (that is, half-termly), with suggestions about how they could provide support for the pupil.

3. The competitive nature of human beings is constantly searching for evidence: that the object of the search is so elusive is something which is not often appreciated or understood, and this misunderstanding can be pernicious for the whole community.

4. The effect of such competition on the school and home life of young people can be immense, ranging from, on the one hand triumph, to apathy and despair on the other, with the attitudes and behaviour which so frequently result. Underlying assumptions include those associated with relativism: pupils' progress is compared with those around, rather than being judged on individual effort.

It is interesting, for example, to reflect on how far the notion of competition is likely to increase the standard of work of pupils. There is little evidence to support any such claims. What seems more likely is that many young people will decide, for numerous reasons, not all academic, that they are not part of these competitions, and with wisdom. And yet such beliefs seem to underlie the following statement, giving details of what type of information school reports should contain:

> ... comparison between the individual's results in examinations and national tests with those of others in the same group, and the national average. (Note 1, p. 135, p. 8).

The question remains, of course, as to what happens to those who *are unable to achieve average attainment*, or even those who are 'average' attainers and who are pressurised to become 'above average'. Assumptions concerning 'average' assume that there will be some above the middle, and some below, whilst the latter are given every incentive (perhaps of the 'stick-and-carrot' variety, such as certificates and trophies) to improve, thus raising the elusive 'average' measurement. Because of the very concept of 'average', there is created a hierarchical system.

We are not advocating the abolition of testing and assessment of pupils' achievements, but what we are advocating is that the methods used for encouraging progress are broadened to take account of personality differences, varieties of temperaments, and recognition given to individuality, which may not neatly fit conventional methods of assessment and examination.

The National Curriculum Council (Note 1, p. 135) sets out the type of detail which the school report should include:

- comments on the pupil's progress in National Curriculum subjects;

- the pupil's level of attainment in each subject at the end of each Key Stage following statutory assessment at ages 7, 11, 14, and 16;

- results of other examinations or tests taken during the year;

- comments on the pupil's achievements in other subjects beside those of the National Curriculum, and in other activities;

- comparison between the individual's results in examinations and national tests with those of others in the same group, and the national average;

- a comment from the Headteacher or class teacher on general progress and attendance record;

- an indication of the person to whom the parent should talk to discuss the report, and details of how to fix an appointment.

There follow a few activities which are designed to encourage the reader to enter into the debate about school reports, written in the light of the above guidelines.

Here is a copy of a school report for a student aged thirteen years, four months. Maureen is a pupil in the secondary phase of her education, in which she has completed one year's work. It is the policy of this High School to provide parents with reports to ensure that they 'know how they are getting on'. Please analyse the details, and offer your interpretation against the following criteria:

- How far does the report follow current guidelines?

- What picture will Maureen's parents be likely to form of their daughter's achievements?

- What effect is the report likely to have on Maureen's future work at the school?

- Do you feel that additional criteria ought to be added to provide a fuller assessment of Maureen's attainments within the 'context' of education, as described above? If so, what would you suggest?

Can you suggest which of the '-isms' described in earlier chapters are

128

Subject	Exam. Mark	Comments
Religious Education	C 41/50	Could be more energetic in oral work.
English	C 118/200	Has quite a good imagination and can express herself fluently. Written work is neat but needs more confidence in oral work.
History	C 20/50	Slow to discuss but interested.
Geography	C 18/50	Works fairly well.
Mathematics	C 45/100	Works much too slowly. When she listens and exerts herself she can do quite well. Poor figures reduce the quality of her work.
Science	C 26/50	Works steadily but records need care.
Needlework	C 64/100	Maureen works quietly but could put more effort into this work.
Art	C 30/50	Always seems interested in her work.
Music	C	More effort is needed.
Physical Education	B	Is a keen, willing worker, showing improvement, especially in games.
Domestic Science	C 64/100	Maureen works well, but could take a more active part in lessons.

A School Report

Key: A = Exceptionally Good B = Above Average C = Satisfactory
D = Not Good Enough E = Unsatisfactory

Number in form: 30   Position in Form: 7

Possible mark: 800   Actual mark: 456.

General Report. Maureen is usually quiet and reserved in school. There is only a slow response to any question put to her personally and I would like to see a change here and to see her join more actively in the doings of other girls. She has improved her form position by *three* places.

influential in the minds of those who wrote the report?

In the opinion of the writers, this report goes much of the way towards fulfilling the requirements set out in the official NCC criteria given above, excepting that some indication needs to be given of the levels of attainment reached in the National Curriculum. Apart from this omission, all would appear to be well.

Alas, however! It may come as a surprise to the reader that this Report was actually written thirty-four years ago, and the fact that it goes so far towards meeting modern criteria might reflect a good deal about current educational thinking and planning and attempts to 'go back to basics'.

If the 'context' of education is to be taken at all seriously, the writers feel that this Report reveals really serious problems, in that the teachers do not – perhaps because of the educational system both past and present – understand the motivation of this student at all. For example, assessment and examination is on the basis of relativist assumptions: how does the student compare with others? Her relative performance is the sole criterion for assessment, and judgement is made accordingly.

Although purporting to be examination marks, only a few of the marks given were for written examinations, namely English, Mathematics, History and Geography. The other marks provided were numerical assessments made by the teacher, and yet both sets of 'marks' were added to provide the total. This was not explained to the parents, and grave misunderstandings could have arisen as a result. In fact, this aspect of the Report alone makes it equal the absurdity of the Red Queen's orders for executions which one reads about in *Alice in Wonderland*!

Many of the teachers pointed to Maureen as being very reserved, and somewhat lazy: for example, the teachers of Religious Education, Mathematics, Music, and History. In fact, because of the specialisation and numbers of children taught by each member of staff, it is unlikely that many of them would know Maureen; one is left suspecting that they read what others had put, and followed suit. The exception is the games mistress, who knew Maureen well since she was a member of the junior hockey team.

The 'General Report' is particularly significant. Maureen is, basically, criticised for being an individual! She must not think in depth in school, apparently, since 'a slow response' to questions indicates laziness; she must, in addition, 'join in the doings of other girls'. The reason is not given. It is quite probable that Maureen is actually puzzling to her teachers, who recognised her individuality but could not understand it.

The alphabetical gradings are not at all helpful. What is 'average'? What does 'satisfactory' mean? There is a total confusion, and in addition the proliferation of 'C' grades would indicate that the teachers took refuge in a safe option, not really being in a position to assess the work and achievement of the pupil in question.

Many more points could be raised in objection to such a Report as this, and examples of such are only too easy to produce. What is of interest is that, if the Report is read very carefully, it is clear that some of the teachers were really interested in Maureen, but had no means of expressing this interest. She was obviously thoughtful, hesitant about discussing ideas which she had not had time to think through thoroughly, imaginative and able to express her ideas in words better than orally.

However, the comments of the teachers – indeed the focus of the Report – related to subject expertise, or lack of it, and these were the details which were stressed, presumably with a view to encouraging the girl to work much harder. The emphasis given to her having 'improved her form position by three places' is, in fact, a 'stick-and-carrot' approach, the carrot being the possibility of improving the position by seven places next time around. What kind of form it was, however, was not disclosed!

No one, it seems, had managed to penetrate the motivation of the student, and what it was that excited her imagination. Overall, the emerging picture is of a reserved, shy girl, approaching adolescence, who is sensitive and thoughtful, and who has interests in things which are not within the orbit of her peers. What, one wonders, might they have been? How could teachers have helped her thinking deepen more, and her skills in communication diversify and develop? What ought to have been teaching points for the future became points of criticism!

It is not difficult to understand why teachers are encouraged to use such report forms, and to develop methods of assessment, recording, and examinations within a framework which is structured against a background of developmental psychology. This way of attempting to organise the educational process is the one within which every citizen has been nurtured. It has become so much a part of society's structure that it is virtually impossible to stand outside of it, view it disinterestedly, and consider whether the possibility exists for an alternative method which could be successful and more reflective of how young people learn, and what is of importance.

The points made about Maureen's school Report are extremely significant here. The remarks – examples of which are written by teachers continually – lean towards the superficial, are confined to subject areas, and give little indication of how the girl will be helped to progress in the future, even of how her parents could assist her at home. Where remarks were made concerning her personality, it is obvious that the teachers had not managed to glimpse any deeper than surface appearances, and what they did perceive was reported in critical, even sarcastic terms.

If assessment, examinations, and school records are to be made in ways which are important, about things which really matter, it is necessary for much reflection in depth concerning what it is that education is attempting to do. If it is in the business of stimulating competition, there are certain to be numerous losers – the vast majority of the population, in fact – and what is likely to happen to them?

Dual standards operate at levels which can evade perception so easily, except by the pupils themselves. How common it is to see competitive matches, often of football or netball, where the players are told it is the game which counts, not whether one's team wins or loses, and yet the losing team has to stand and watch its conqueror being presented with a large silver cup! On the same subject, pupils are frequently told that a particular sport is a team event – every player is important – and then a teacher suddenly announces a 'boy/girl of the match' award!

Such deception is easily recognised, with the result that pupils tend to 'opt out' of their schooling from quite an early age, turning instead to their interests outside school which go largely unrecognised. One part of life seems not to enrich the other, and many adolescents seem relieved when they reach the last day of their formal schooling.

From 1993, OFSTED has been evaluating schools' provision for the 'spiritual, moral, mental, cultural and physical development' of pupils (its central aim) and its effectiveness in the life of the school. What is of grave concern, however, is the apparent split between this central aim of education and the assessment and testing which will be carried out in subject areas, but which does not, apparently, comment on the personality development of individual pupils as a result of their learning.

A useful task is to design a record sheet for Maureen, and complete it according to the following criteria which relate to personal development, together with those provided by the NCC on p. 127, using Maureen's Report as evidence of her performance and achievement in school.

- Develop the capacity to reflect.

- As a result of increasing reflection, discuss ideas with others.

- Show through written or spoken ideas a growing awareness of the inter-relatedness of ideas.

The Record Sheet given below is offered as a suggestion. Does the form you devised and completed for Maureen paint her character and personality development in a more positive light than the school Report which is printed on page 128? We would make the following points:

- Maureen's potential is very promising; at the moment she shows herself to be very thoughtful, to the extent of appearing to be on a different mental plane from others.

- She needs to be given space and time to develop her ideas, and encouragement to share these in discussion.

- Much of her energy goes into reflective thought; the probability of original thinking is quite strong, and should be encouraged, especially by learning to recognise the relationships between ideas and the phenomena of life generally.

The approaches to assessment and reporting on pupils' progress as argued for above are, unfortunately, unlikely to be used in the near future: all new ideas

RECORD SHEET		
Name . . . . Date of birth		
Key: * = early stages $\quad\quad$ + = development taking place § = complex development $\quad$ # = high levels of achievement		
Develop the capacity to reflect	+	
As a result of increasing reflection, discuss ideas with others	*	
Show through written or spoken ideas, a growing awareness of the inter-relationships of ideas	+	

GENERAL COMMENTS
Maureen is a thoughtful pupil who needs to be given time and space in which
to develop her potential for reflective thinking. She shows promise in
expressing her ideas in writing, and has to be allowed time to develop this
interest. Her thought is, at this time, rather deeper than that of others, and she
must be given freedom to develop her individuality. Unlike many pupils, her
written work is in advance of her conversational skills.

PLANS FOR FUTURE DEVELOPMENT
Maureen needs to be introduced to a wide range of literature to enrich her
developing imaginative powers, and time in which to reflect on them. Some
work on the use of metaphor in language could be introduced.

take some considerable time to become accepted within conventional systems. In the meantime, however, the writers feel it to be realistic to produce the type of report reproduced on page 134. In the interim, how can this be done without causing too much damage to pupils such as Maureen? We suggest that the following guidelines may be helpful for readers to follow when faced with such a daunting and unrealistic task (see also page 134):

1. Wherever possible, emphasise positive points, such as thoughtfulness, humour, enthusiasm, liveliness, or determination.

2. In order to stimulate progress, wherever possible mention anything which the pupil has done which bodes well for the future.

3. Under all subjects, try to make general points which will increase the pupil's confidence, rather than cause misery or defiance.

3. Do everything possible to help the pupil understand that the school is on his/her side, and is fully sympathetic to the problems faced.

4. Suggest ways in which the pupil, and parents, could help performance, and make suggestions about what is planned for future lessons. Bearing these points in mind, we now suggest that the reader might like to write *positive* points against each of the subject headings, and write a General Report which could encourage this pupil in her future lessons at the school.

What about Maureen's future? It could go forward in at least two ways, especially when she has to take public examinations such as GCSE. With encouragement, especially by boosting her confidence in mathematics, she could well train for teaching, but the fact that she will need to record a pass in mathematics in order to enter the profession could be a hurdle. If teachers continually fail to understand how she is motivated, and make negative comments in the process, she could easily become dispirited and give up trying altogether. What would you yourself predict? There can be little doubt that the school report which pupils take home has great importance for how their parents perceive their school work, and the attitudes which they themselves adopt for school life generally.

Conclusion

The questions surrounding the phenomena of testing, assessing and examining need clarification at depth. It would be useful to begin by questioning how far 'stage theories' derived from developmental psychology continue to dominate our assumptions concerning what should be tested, assessed and examined, and the likely effects on both students, children and their parents. Thought should then be given to possible alternative ways in which education could develop which aim to:

● allow children and students freedom to pursue their own interests and

We suggest something along these lines:

Subject	Comments
Religious Education	Is extremely thoughtful. She has much to offer by way of new ideas.
English Level 4	Is very imaginative and has a very interesting style in written work.
History Level 5	Shows much interest and is keen.
Geography Level 4	Work is neat and thoughtful.
Mathematics Level 4	Works slowly because of her thoughtfulness.
Science Level 4	Concentrates well and is curious.
Needlework Level 4	Is quiet and thoughtful.
Art Level 4	Enjoys herself.
CDT Level 4	Is interested in sorting through paintings of early periods, e.g. icons and illuminations. Enjoys experimenting with oils.
Music Level 4	Enjoys close harmony singing, and listening to choral music.
Games & PE Level 4	Is a member of junior hockey team; very enthusiastic and plays hockey every Saturday morning voluntarily.
Cookery Level 4	Has a sense of humour.

General Report. Maureen is a very thoughtful pupil, and we intend to introduce her to exciting literature, such as 'Wuthering Heights' and 'Jane Eyre' next term. She has a quiet sense of humour, and relaxes by playing hockey with her friends during breaks, lunchtimes and Saturday mornings.

develop positive personality traits through areas which interest them;

- assess, and examine, children's and student's achievements according to criteria which avoid narrow bias;

- provide records and reports for parents which encourage positive thinking based on increasing curiosity and creativity, rather than individual or corporate competitive attitudes.

We would describe such approaches to education as Personality Centred, rather than Progressive or Child Centred, as they recognise as their central drive individuality, the complexity of the human mind and the need to allow young people the opportunity of developing their interests in depth through a system which is respectful of personal autonomy and freedom, working and developing through subject disciplines.

Note

National Curriculum Council (1992) *Starting Out with the National Curriculum* (NCC).

Chapter 11

The Question of Discipline

If assessment is one of the teacher's biggest bugbears, discipline is perhaps number one anxiety in many schools, and not just for young, inexperienced teachers. Discipline is increasingly identified as being urgent if the young are to be kept in control and society in reasonable order. Those who feel most in harmony with the kinds of assumptions and values concerning education argued for in this book may well be the most perturbed at the thought of unruly classrooms, complaints from parents and other teachers, and the accusation of a *laissez-faire* approach which treats schooling as play.

Skills of a high order are required to build up the sense of self-discipline essential for any education worthy of the name (according to the discussion in Chapter 3) – and able to promote the personality development which is the real purpose of assessment procedures as outlined in Chapter 10.

The purpose of this chapter is to discuss how to make the crucial link between school/classroom experience and the development of self-discipline in children.

A brief historical excursion

'Fetch that stool,' said Mr Brocklehurst, pointing to a very high one from which a monitor had just risen: it was brought.
'Place the child upon it.'
And I was placed there, by whom I don't know. I was in no condition to note particulars. I was only aware that they had hoisted me up to the height of Mr Brocklehurst's nose, that he was within a yard of me, and that a spread of shot orange and purple silk pelisses, and a cloud of silvery plumage extended and waved below me. (Note 1, p. 147 p. 73)

As those familiar with the story of *Jane Eyre* will know, there followed a full description of how the child was disciplined by being humiliated before her peers and forced to stand on the stool for half an hour whilst other members of her class went to and fro about their work. We are told that the reason for the punishment was that Jane had told a lie, and the procedures followed by

Mr Brocklehurst would, no doubt, have two main reasons – that is two reasons as *consciously* recognised by him, which were:

1. to dissuade other pupils from telling lies;
2. to dissuade Jane Eyre from telling lies in the future.

However, Charlotte Brontë makes it quite plain to the reader that other motivations were at work, the main ones, perhaps, being:

1. Mr Brocklehurst used the pupils at the school as vessels through which his own cruelty could be given full vent;
2. Mr Brocklehurst resented the way money was spent on the orphaned pupils: his charity was extremely cold;
3. discipline was seen – at least in Victorian England – as a means by which adult values were imposed upon the young.

The development of the English educational system, and adult perceptions of the children for whom it has been devised, are reflected by the form which discipline took during any particular period. The further back one looks the harsher the methods used seem to be – caning, tawse, humiliation – all of these elements were familiar to pupils in English schools until fairly recent decades. *The Concise Oxford Dictionary* provides the following definitions of discipline:

> Branch of instruction: mental & moral training . . . system of rules for conduct; control extended over members of a Church; chastisement; mortification by penance. *As a verb*: bring under control, train to obedience & order.

What these definitions have in common is that they all see discipline as something to be enforced, or imposed, to ensure that order is maintained. In addition to the above, the following definition is revelatory:

> . . . order maintained among schoolboys, soldiers, prisoners, etc.

Why should schoolboys (or indeed schoolgirls) be included among soldiers and prisoners? Responses to this question no doubt embrace the following:

- all the individuals within the groups have been brought together with a common purpose: soldiers to learn to fight; prisoners in order to curtail their liberty; schoolchildren in order to be educated;

- all the groups have the potential to be unruly;

- all the individuals within the groups will be expected to conform to some form of 'authority' which knows better than they themselves do concerning what is needed for 'the good of society'.

Regarding education, and as far as Victorian England (and much of the twentieth century) was concerned, the main reason for providing education was to ensure that the population was at least basically literate and numerate in order to cope with newly developing forms of employment which required additional skills to those associated with agricultural work, industrial labour and the domestic industry. The role of the adult world was to ensure that its own values were impressed upon the young and immature.

A vivid description of the results of this philosophy and how it affected the pupils in a primary school in an industrial area is provided by D.H. Lawrence in the following extracts from *The Rainbow*. Before beginning her career as an elementary school teacher, Ursula Brangwen dreamed

> ... how she would make the little, ugly children love her. She would be so *personal*. Teachers were always so hard and impersonal. There was no vivid relationship. She would make everything personal and vivid, she would give herself, she would give, give, give all her great stores of wealth to her children. (Note 2, p. 147, p. 367)

However, things did not go as Ursula had planned. Her love and the 'giving of herself' resulted in her being stoned on her way to the bus stop after school, and the gradual deterioration of the pupils' work. Lawrence blamed the system: the classes in schools were too large, and kindness and sympathy were considered by the pupils to reveal a weak person whom they were only too eager to exploit for their own amusement. This is why Ursula found herself compelled to play the rules which the system had evolved, and which demanded *discipline*:

> The children had forced her to the beatings. No, she did not pity them. She had come to them full of kindness and love, and they would have torn her to pieces. (p. 405)

Discipline in schools today

Although the forms of discipline which are described in the extracts from literature are unlikely to be found in schools in England and Wales today, the assumptions on which the educational system itself is based are not too different from the ones experienced by Charlotte Brontë in the early decades of the nineteenth century or those known to Lawrence in the early twentieth: pupils are brought together in large numbers in order that they should be educated, and education itself seems to be conceived as the acquisition of knowledge and skills. Perhaps both Brontë and Lawrence, if they were able to enter the classroom of the average school today, would be struck by a greater informality in approaches to discipline, mainly characterised by desks and tables arranged in groups rather than in rows; less rote learning and more general freedom of movement around the classroom. However, such visible evidence can be misleading. What we see in schools is a system which has developed over many decades – even centuries – and which carries with it certain basic assumptions of what it is that education is trying to achieve, and the means by which this can be accomplished.

We invite readers to tease out the values held by Mr Brocklehurst, and the assumptions behind the various dictionary definitions, and contrast these with the values of Ursula Brangwen before harsh experience pushed her into a more rigid traditional approach – an experience reproduced thousands of times when the idealism of student-teachers gets knocked out of them in the rough realities of actual life in school.

It would seem that the underlying assumptions concerning discipline focus on the importance of order for the maintenance of a healthy society, and the necessity to subject the young to the dictates of adults 'who know best' as the means of achieving this end. Discipline, from the early days of education, has been an attempt to train pupils to behave in ways thought to be beneficial, and has been enforced through the carrot-or-stick approach.

The stick part of this used to include corporal punishment if necessary. Corporal punishment is no longer legal in state schools in this country, but that has certainly not meant the demise of the assumption behind the stick-or-carrot way of impressing the desired values on pupils

Because of this continuity in assumptions and values many see the answer to the discipline problems of today as lying in a return to 'traditional methods'. Progressive trends such as those argued for by Blenkein and Kelly (Note 3, p. 147) – and other theorists who are sympathetically disposed to the ideas of Rousseau and Piaget – are equally unlikely to effect successful learning in the classroom or elsewhere. This is because of the serious under-estimation of the ability of pupils which underlies such psychology (see Chapter 8 for a full discussion of this). The historical context within which Rousseau wrote *Emile* – that is in Pre-Revolutionary France – is not usually fully explored by theorists who are keen to apply such ideas to much later developments in education.

Such an attempted return to former modes of operating discipline can only prove counterproductive in the long run. John Wilson (Note 4, p. 147) explains why. His theory concerning ways in which pupils may be enabled to consider moral issues could well be applied across the whole arena of school life, including discipline. Wilson (pp. 31–2) describes two aspects of moral education, one of which he calls 'Identification with Authority' (pp. 14–17). Here the individual sees him/herself as the recipient of a code of values which require to be adopted, and according to which it is desirable to live one's life. Such values are passed from one generation to the next. Wilson goes on to outline one of the results – which is probably all too common in every classroom in every school in the country – of this system when pupils do not 'identify' with the values being passed on. This he calls 'rejection of authority', and it is characterised by efforts on the part of the pupil to rebel against the values being encouraged. The results of this rejection take many forms: they may be straight-forward 'anti-social' (that is, anti-social according to the values rejected) forms of behaviour, manipulation of the system (which happened in the case of the Self-Manager Scheme described in Chapter 2) or even aggression and violence.

Examples of ways in which 'authority' frequently tries to persuade pupils to adopt, rather than reject, the values being presented include force (in the past, corporal punishment); reward systems (e.g. team points, the

Self-Manager Scheme), or even bribery (e.g. the giving of sweets, personal privileges) in return for an acceptance of 'correct values'.

The assumption that large numbers of young children will require some form of externally-enforced discipline underlies many of the approaches to the administration of schools and contributes, to a great extent, to the disciplinary problems found within them. What seems to be the problem is the whole conception of what education ought to be trying to achieve.

Education itself as discipline

It would seem that much in-depth thought is urgently required concerning the educational system and what it is that schools are required to achieve. What is required is a deeper appreciation of the word 'education', as argued for in Chapter 3, and on this basis what changes are needed if what is commonly found to be happening in the classroom can be accurately called 'education'.

There is, however, an alternative way of viewing discipline, which is that *education in itself* should be a form of discipline, rather than something which is impossible unless *linked with it*. This view conceives of discipline rather differently from those who voted to install the Self-Manager Scheme which was described in Chapter 2. Although purporting to encourage self-reliance, the scheme was really a disguised way of imposing adult ideas upon the young, and pupils were quick to spot this and exploit the system to their own advantage.

The concept of education outlined in Chapter 3 sees all aspects of personality development, and ultimately, therefore, the wellbeing of society, as being the goal of education, and this is to be achieved partly through the medium of subject content but also by the general ethos of the school – that is the values which are transmitted to pupils both in and outside the classroom.

This understanding is revolutionary in its implications because, perhaps for the first time in the history of the educational system, the idea that *the subject is to be taught to serve the pupil* has been made the reason for educational provision. The importance for the role of discipline is enormous since the subject itself should become disciplinary. Whether one is being taught mathematics, science, history or any other subject, what should be acquired through the very act of study are reasoned assumptions according to which values will develop and which in turn depend upon the depth of thought which has been reached when following any particular discipline.

However, it is not only through subject areas in schools that personality development is effected, but also through the attitudes, assumptions and general ethos of the whole school community.

The reason why the Self-Manager Scheme is non-educational (see Chapter 2) is because no attempts were made to help the individuals concerned to think for themselves and reasons – which is the basis for true education. Wilson

(Note 4, p. 147, p. 36) argues with conviction that education should appeal to the human capacity to *reason*. He writes:

> Clearly, any development of a potentially rational creature from birth to adulthood faces this general problem (i.e. that personal autonomy is abrogated by the authority of parents, teacher, etc.).

The entire educational system – and ideally the family – will need to identify as its priority the development of this 'potential for rationalism' – that is enabling the pupil to think through his/her problem, arriving at decisions and, perhaps, solutions in the general understanding that:

> his/her own particular views, feelings and commitments must take second place to the overall procedures of reason, even when – particularly when – his/her feelings are especially passionate. (p. 42)

Thus, discipline enters into every aspect of education, whether in the home or school, but discipline under this definition is rather different from the official definitions given above. It becomes so closely perceived as education that the two become one, and the goal is (see Wilson) the attainment of true personal autonomy based on the development of cognitive reasoning.

Regarding the latter, education should take place within the classroom, corridor, washroom, cloakroom, yard, playing field, during school outings, or during any situation when there is interaction between teacher and pupil.

The same applies for the secondary school. The whole gamut of activities, including extra-curricular, and the attitudes promoted by the staff as a whole, either help or hinder the crucial building up of student self-responsibility.

Discipline in schools, particularly in the secondary phase, can be a real problem and to a large extent is reflective of society as a whole, that is, of attitudes associated with consumerism, materialism, positivism and other members of that family. Nevertheless, it remains essential that order must prevail in schools if effective learning is to take place. Figure 11.1 provides some guidelines for teachers in the secondary phase especially those who, each week, and even sometimes each day, are faced with classes of young people with whom they have limited contact, perhaps as little as thirty-five minutes a week, and whom it is, therefore, impossible to know.

We suggest that the reader might like to comment on the following remarks, making mention of the particular assumptions held by the speaker concerning the nature of education:

- 'Jennifer, if you don't work to pass your 'A' levels, you've completely wasted your time in school.'

- 'If you don't get those sums done right now, you needn't expect to be playing in the cricket team tonight.'

- 'Will you put your mind on that book you are supposed to be reading? You have another half hour with me before you get technology, and you are going to work in it.'

The Teacher: needs to

*be oneself;
*avoid role play;
*avoid gimmicks, e.g. language, dress;
*maintain a sense of humour;
*be sympathetic;
*be well prepared;
*avoid aimless discussion/ confrontation;
*be honest;
*share the problems to be overcome with students.

Communication Skills:

*eye-contact;
*smiling;
*facial expression generally;
*physical stance;
*movements;
*show interest in students

MAINTAINING ORDER IN THE SECONDARY CLASSROOM

The Work: should:

*be planned by the students within the parameters agreed with the teacher;
*be flexible, i.e. allow scope for development in new directions;
*be directed towards set goals;
*reflect some method of assessment;
*be recorded;
*include some form of student evaluation.

The Student: needs

*To build up a reasonable image of him/herself;
*to take responsibility for his/her learning;
*to learn how to develop ideas;
*advice concerning developing work, materials, to solve problems, both practical and otherwise; *to be active.

Figure 11.1   The classroom merry-go-round

In the light of these discussions, such statements as the following (which are too frequently heard in schools) are revealing concerning teachers' perceptions of the role of schools:

Anthony will never be ready for the comprehensive in September.

On analysis, this statement reveals the following assumptions:

1. that the function of the primary school is to prepare pupils for the comprehensive school;
2. that there exists some 'set standard' which individuals must attain in order to be suitable for comprehensive education;
3. that achievement is connected with age;
4. that there is no place for individuality in education.

If the requirements of the 'context' of the National Curriculum are to be addressed, a much more informed, flexible attitude towards the individual will require to be developed.

Focus on the school: non-subject situations

Below, a classroom situation is given which demands an immediate response from the teacher, and possibilities of how this could be made. We suggest that each response is analysed according to the following points, and noted for future reference:

1. What would motivate the teacher to make the response?
2. What would motivate the pupil in each instance to behave as described?
3. What effect would each possible response have upon the pupil's personality development?
4. How far would each possible response help the pupil concerned to reason, as defined above?
5. How far would each possible response encourage:

    i) personal identification (unquestioning acceptance);

    ii) rebellion.

Please add any additional responses which you can construct, and evaluate them.

The Scissors Game

A group of Year 3 children are using scissors during lesson time. Lisa comes to you, holding a piece of hair which, she claims, Susan has just cut from her (Lisa's) head. She is worried that she will get into trouble at home. What will you do?

1. send both of the children to the Headteacher;
2. send a note to the parents, including (for Susan's), the cut hair;

144

3. At the end of the session after the other children have gone from the room, find out exactly what happened. Try to establish whether the act was *i)* mischievous; *ii)* done in temper; *iii)* done as a 'dare'; *iv)* done deliberately to upset Susan and get her into trouble. Explain why her parents will have to be told about it and why they will be upset. Report the incident to the Headteacher before you go home;

4. ask the class for witnesses, and shout at the culprit;

5. give the whole class a lecture on what scissors should be used for;

6. forbid both of the children involved to use scissors for the rest of term.

Incidents such as the one above, provide opportunities for teachers to help the children concerned to learn how to think reflectively. Such incidents are rarely recognised as possessing potential for helping forward children's thinking capacity and associated personality development. Indeed, experience has indicated that such incidents are usually considered to be a nuisance which take up a great deal of the teaching day.

As discussed, however, the astute teacher will, whenever possible, use every chance which comes along to help the children to practise their thinking skills. Education is not confined to the classroom: it could take place during every waking hour of each individual's life. Events like this frequently occur with this age group. To warn the children beforehand that no such cutting should take place is both dogmatic and likely to provide them with naughty ideas!

1. uneducational.

2. uneducational.

3. This response encourages the children to reflect on their actions, and the effects which they have on other people. It is important to establish the motive here, in case other incidents of naughtiness could be related, and could be examples of bullying. It is important that the Headteacher should be informed of what had taken place in case of complaints by parents.

4. uneducational.

5. uneducational.

6. uneducational, and in addition would be extremely difficult to enforce. The children may need to use scissors as part of their work.

The criteria for selecting responses – in any situations in school or outside it, e.g. on outings – should always be:

- How far would my action deepen the child's thought?

- What kind of personality development would be likely to result?

- How far would the response address the context of education?

If discipline is understood to be synonymous with the educational process, and concerned with individuality, dogmatism must be rejected, with, ideally, a commensurate reduction in rebellious responses from pupils.

Subject teaching as a discipline

Discipline in schools is commonly perceived as being something which is distinct from the learning process itself, and yet which is a necessary condition if learning is to take place. Thus, if 'Discipline' appears on the agenda for staff meetings, it is most unlikely that anyone would expect to discuss lesson content under that item. True discipline has profound effects upon general personality development over considerable periods of time, and has a positive focus. It is more likely to develop from personal engagement with situations as described above, and from lesson content which stimulates reflective thought and discussion, than it is from staff efforts to settle children in class and to deal with personal complaints and confrontations before teaching and learning can take place.

How does discipline operate through subject areas in ways which help children's overall development? First, any lesson must comprise material which is presented in ways likely to engage the interests of children. It must also contain material which, even if remote in time and place from personal experience, helps illuminate the everyday events of pupils' lives. Such material, particularly, though not exclusively, for young children, emphasises the abstract emotions which are common to humanity throughout all ages and all geographical regions.

As an example of how such ideas work, please refer to Figure 11.2 which provides suggestions of how to plan a scheme of work which relates the lesson content to pupils' spiritual, moral and emotional needs. Having studied the material provided here, we suggest readers might like either to choose a story which they have used with pupils, or to select one from the following, and plan a scheme of work which aims to help pupils think rationally about emotion.

Aesop's Fable: The Wind and the Sun;
Androcles and the Lion;
Little Red Riding Hood.

Such studies and discussions with pupils become disciplinary and educational because of the thought concerning the human condition which they stimulate. To feel the pain of jealousy, or to endure the results of the jealousy of another without being helped to rationalise what is happening can only, except in exceptional cases, leave pupils at the mercy of whatever experiences happened to be encountered. However, in time, it is through understanding that self-discipline will take form: not because it is forced to happen but because reason directs the intellect within a framework of rational thought which is self-sustaining in times of crisis.

146

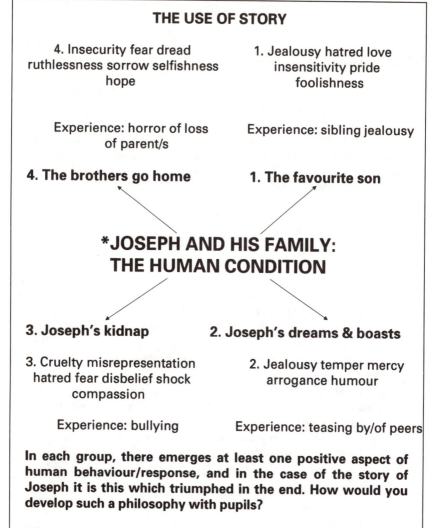

Figure 11.2 Thinking about emotions: the use of story

Summary

This chapter has discussed in some detail various definitions of 'discipline' in order to clarify thought concerning its relationship with education: whether what is commonly defined as 'discipline' is actually something distinct from education, or whether the word signifies something which masquerades as discipline (as understood in an educational context) but which is quite distinct from it and which works in opposition.

Definitions of discipline which continue to dominate the world of education are as found in dictionaries. It would seem, however, that current legislation from central government sees education generally as having a radically different purpose: that of personal development in its various aspects.

In this context, education must become a form of discipline in itself, which works through the entire school day, both inside and outside the classroom, within lesson content and all other situations which develop: all need to be seen as educational opportunities. How this could be done has been demonstrated by practical examples drawn from school experience.

However, if 'education through discipline' is to be a living reality within the educational system, it will be necessary for much further research into the assumptions which underlie the present system. It would seem that to change these dramatically would be to bring about a worthwhile educational revolution.

Notes and References

1. Brontë, C. (1918) *Jane Eyre*, Collins.
2. Lawrence, D. H. (1973) *The Rainbow*, Penguin.
3. Blenkein, and Kelly (1989) *The Primary Curriculum*, Routledge.
4. Wilson, J. (1990) *An Introduction to Moral Education*, Cassell.

National Curriculum Council (1993) *Moral and Spiritual Development – A Discussion Paper*.

Postscript

The Necessity for Education in Beliefs and Values

Every citizen has some personal experience upon which to draw when making assumptions about education. The effectiveness of that experience can be judged according to how far one is able to think logically and critically on the basis of evidence and draw appropriate conclusions.

In the cases of Colin and Caroline, with which this book began, difficulties began to emerge in their responses to education before the end of the primary school. The two young men who died in the car crash (also Chapter 1) had become victims on a rather different plane, but victims nonetheless of the confused beliefs and values within which society attempts to operate.

We suggest that the reader might like to reflect on how education could have helped these young people to think clearly about their own beliefs and values and by so doing evaluate their personal priorities.

To answer this question it is vital that many penetrating questions are asked about the assumptions which form the basis for the society itself. This necessitates investigating whether there is evidence to support the theory that the empirical realm could be underpinned by a framework of reality which itself transcends empirical analysis.

In Chapters 4 and 5, how this investigation can be attempted was discussed, and its implications for both education and the assumptions one makes about life generally were presented in succeeding chapters. How can the school community hope to address such a huge task? The answer, of course, lies in the beliefs and values according to which the school operates, for it is undeniably true that if one – whether teacher or pupil – anticipates rebellion, such will take place.

The following outline of an ideal school might produce at least three possible reactions:

1. it is ludicrous because so far removed from reality;

2. it does not reflect what pupils from the real world are like;

3. it *must* happen – or be approached – if schools are to become truly educational establishments.

An Ideal School		
Appearance	Atmosphere	Integrity
visually attractive; free from litter and clutter; areas set aside for working and exploring.	lively but orderly; emphasis on the individual; time available daily for free-choice work.	discussion of controversial issues which gets beyond the superficial; all areas of the curriculum enjoying equal status.
Staff	Head	Pupils
awareness of influence of speech, dress, etc.; leading without being pompous or dogmatic; avoidance of critical attitudes of others.	enthusiastic; open to ideas; prepared to make decisions; avoidance of having favourites/enemies; supportive of staff.	self-motivated; learning to plan some of their own activities; friendly; well motivated.
Methods of Teaching	*Organisation*	Discipline
varied throughout day; individuality valued; flexible.	minimum meetings; minimum ill-feeling; no permanent hierarchy; openness to suggestions; frequent outside visits.	uniform; reason/justice; work targets; humour.

Overall, we stress the importance of a system of education which has as its cornerstone a commitment to help pupils to discriminate between the conflicting values which operate so pervasively throughout society. For such a system to be effective, education in beliefs and values will need to infiltrate every element of school life, both within lessons and outside them.

We conclude by asking readers to reflect on a remark once overheard in the playground of a primary school overshadowed by dilapidated Edwardian housing:

What I like about this school is the people. I hate the buildings around here, but inside you get a good feeling – like you really matter and belong.

Recommended Reading

Educational

Carr, David (1991) Education and values, *British Journal of Educational Studies*, vol 39, August 1991.

Claxton, Guy (1990) *Teaching to Learn: a direction for education*, Cassell.

Fisher, Robert (1990) *Teaching Children to Think*, Basil Blackwell.

Habgood, John (1990) Are moral values enough?, *British Journal of Educational Studies*, vol 38 no.2, May 1990.

Hansen, David T. (1993) The moral importance of the teacher's style, *Journal of Curriculum Studies*, vol. 25, no.5.

Harris, M. (1988) *Women and Teaching*, Paulist Press.

Haydon, Graham (1993/4) Moral education, *Philosophy Now*, Winter 1993/4.

Kirby, Dan and Kuykendall, Carol (1991) *Mind Matters: teaching for thinking* Boynton/Cook, Heinemann.

Lawton, Denis (1989) *Education, Culture & the National Curriculum*, Hodder & Stoughton.

Lipman, Matthew (1991) *Thinking and Education*, Cambridge University Press.

Matthews, G.B. (1980) *Philosophy and the Young Child*, Harvard University Press.

Moffett, James (1992) *Harmonic Learning: keynoting school reform* Boynton/Cook, Heinemann.

Newman, Judith M. (ed) (1990) *Finding our own Way: teachers exploring their assumptions*, Heinemann Educational Books.

Plunkett, Dudley (1990) *Secular and Spiritual Values: Grounds for hope in education*, Routledge.

Raths, Louis E., Harmin, Merrill, and Simon, Sidney B. (1978) *Values and Teaching, second edition*, Charles E. Merrill Publishing Co.

Simon, Sidney B., Howe, Leland W., and Kirschenbaum, Howard (1972) *Values Clarification: A handbook of practical strategies for teachers and students*, Hart Publishing Co. Inc.

Tasker, M (1990) Values and Teacher Education, paper produced for *The National Association for Values in Education and Training*, May 1990.

White, Richard, and Gunstone, Richard (1992) *Probing Understanding*, Falmer Press.

Whitehead, A.N. (1970) *The Aims of Education and other Essays*, Macmillan Free Press.

Wilson, J. (1990) *A New Introduction to Moral Education*, Cassell.

General and philosophical

Abbott, E. (1987) *The Story of Flatland*, Penguin.

Barfield, Owen (1971) *What Coleridge Thought,* Wesleyan University Press.

Barnes, Jonathan (1982) *Aristotle*, Oxford University Press.

Borgmann, A. (1991) *Technology and the Character of Contemporary Life: a philosophical inquiry*, University of Chicago Press.

Bronowski, J. and Mazlish, Bruce (1970) *The Western Intellectual Tradition from Leonardo to Hegel*, Pelican.

Capra, F. (1983) *The Turning Point: science, society and the rising culture*, Fontana.

Clarke, Kenneth (1969) *Civilisation*, BBC Books.

Hare, R.M. (1982) *Plato*, Oxford University Press.

Hinman, L.M. (1994) *Ethics: a pluralistic approach to moral theory*, Harcourt Brace College Publishers.

Jencks, Charles (1986) *What is Post-Modernism*? Academy Editions.

MacIntyre, A. (1988) *Whose Justice, Which Rationality*? Duckworth.

McNaughton, (1988) *Moral Vision: An Introduction to Ethics*, Basil Blackwell.

Murdoch, Iris (1992) *Metaphysics as a Guide to Morals*, Penguin Books.

Nagel, Thomas (1987) *What Does It All Mean? A very short introduction to philosophy*, Oxford University Press.

Norris, Christopher (1982) *Deconstruction: Theory and Practice*, Methuen.

Ortony, A. (ed) (1979) *Metaphor and Thought*, Cambridge University Press.

Polanyi, M. (1962) *Personal Knowledge: towards a post-critical philosophy*, Routledge & Kegan Paul.

Raeper, W. and Smith, L. (1991) *A Beginners Guide to Ideas*, Lion.

Sheldrake, Rupert (1994) *Seven Experiments that Could Change the World*, Fourth Estate.

Stewart, Ian (1989) *Does God Play Dice?: the new mathematics of chaos*, Penguin.

Storr, A. (1983) *Jung: selected writings introduced by Anthony Storr*, Fontana.

Trigg, Roger (1980, 2nd edition 1989) *Reality at Risk: a defense of realism in philosophy and the sciences*, Harvester Wheatsheaf.

152

Index

154